Reading Contemporary Society through Editorials

英語社説で読み解く現代社会

Kazuya Yasuhara
Osamu Kito

EIHŌSHA

音声ファイルのダウンロード方法

英宝社ホームページ（http://www.eihosha.co.jp/）の
「テキスト音声ダウンロード」バナーをクリックすると、
音声ファイルダウンロードページにアクセスすることができます。

はしがき

　本書は、*The Japan Times* の社説 (Editorials) の中から、現代社会を象徴する6つの興味深いトピックに焦点をあてて、初級～中級レベルの英語学習者が英文の読解能力を高めていくことができるように教材加工された、リーディングのテキストです。目次にも示されていますが、本書では、「サンゴ礁」「アルファ碁」「高齢者の安全運転」「違法漁業」「軍事目的の研究」「ヒトゲノム」といった多種多様なトピックの英文記事を取り上げており、いずれのトピックも現代社会において何らかの複雑な課題を私たちに提起していると言えます。本書を通して、*The Japan Times* の社説から取られた良質で奥深い英文を味わいながら、私たちの身近に存在している現代社会の諸問題について、じっくりと考えをめぐらせてみる機会にしてみてはいかがでしょうか。

　各ユニットの構成は、下記の通りとなります。

Reading Passage:
　段落ごとにWords, Phrases, Comprehension という学習項目を設定していますので、読解英文の細部にわたるまで、しっかりと学習していくことができます。

Writing Exercises:
　読解教材に登場する語句を参考にしながら、ライティングの基礎を学習していくことができます。学習者の様々なレベルに対応できるように、Phrase Writing とSentence Writingという2つの学習項目を設定しました。

Vocabulary Building:
　現代社会を象徴する重要キーワードを、日英対照式で学習していくことができます。英語フレーズ力の増強にお役立てください。

　最後に、本書の出版に向けて多大なるご尽力を頂きました、英宝社の橋本稔寛氏と下村幸一氏に、この場を借りて、感謝申し上げたいと思います。

2018年4月 名古屋にて
編著者一同

目　次

はしがき ……………………………………………………………… 3

Unit 1	**The Need to Protect Coral Reefs (1)** ……………… 5
	―サンゴ礁の保護対策（1）

Unit 2	**The Need to Protect Coral Reefs (2)** ……………… 13
	―サンゴ礁の保護対策（2）

Unit 3	**AlphaGo AI Stuns Go Community (1)** …………… 21
	―アルファ碁の脅威（1）

Unit 4	**AlphaGo AI Stuns Go Community (2)** …………… 29
	―アルファ碁の脅威（2）

Unit 5	**Safe Driving by Senior Citizens (1)** …………… 37
	―高齢者の安全運転に向けて（1）

Unit 6	**Safe Driving by Senior Citizens (2)** …………… 45
	―高齢者の安全運転に向けて（2）

Unit 7	**Tighten Measures to Combat Illegal Fishing (1)** ………… 55
	―違法漁業への対策強化（1）

Unit 8	**Tighten Measures to Combat Illegal Fishing (2)** ………… 63
	―違法漁業への対策強化（2）

Unit 9	**Scientists and Dual-Use Technologies (1)** ………………… 71
	―科学者と両用技術（1）

Unit 10	**Scientists and Dual-Use Technologies (2)** ………………… 81
	―科学者と両用技術（2）

Unit 11	**Human Genome Editing (1)** …………………………… 89
	―ヒトゲノム編集技術（1）

Unit 12	**Human Genome Editing (2)** …………………………… 99
	―ヒトゲノム編集技術（2）

Unit 1

The Need to Protect Coral Reefs (1)

Reading Passage

1 Coral reefs may not relate to people's daily lives, but their role in nature cannot be dismissed. They provide habitats for various types of animals and offer fishing and tourism resources. They also serve as natural embankments to protect land against big waves, including tsunami. However, the ecosystems that embrace coral reefs are under threat from the serious danger of coral bleaching — apparently due to rising sea water temperatures linked to climate change. The government and the public should realize that a key component of measures to protect coral reefs is the fight against global warming, and act accordingly.

2 According to the Environment Ministry, coral reefs from the Amami Islands of Kagoshima Prefecture to the Yaeyama Islands of Okinawa Prefecture suffered large-scale bleaching last summer. In the Sekisei lagoon lying between Ishigaki Island and Iriomote Island, both in Okinawa, more than 90 percent of the coral was found bleached, and 70 percent of the coral was found to be dead. The ministry says that the current situation affecting coral in the sea off southern Japan is the most serious since large-scale bleaching in 1998. High temperatures prevailed in seawater around the world in 1997 and 1998, killing 16 percent of reef-building coral worldwide.

3 As the extensive coral damage in the late 1990s shows, bleaching of coral reefs is a global phenomenon. The Environment Ministry cites the U.S. National Oceanic and Atmospheric Administration (NOAA) as saying that El Niño events — warming of surface waters and reduced upwelling of cold, nutrient-rich water off the western coast of South America — from 2015 to 2016 have caused unprecedented widespread and long-running coral bleaching, leading to the worst damage ever in the Great Barrier Reef of Australia and Kiribati in the central Pacific Ocean. This coral bleaching mentioned by NOAA continues to this day.

4 The ministry also quotes a report by the Intergovernmental Panel on Climate Change that a rise in seawater temperature by 2 degrees Celsius can cause large-scale coral bleaching every year, inflicting devastating damage to coral reefs.

【335 words—*The Japan Times* (MAY 13, 2017)】

[Notes] El Niño: エル・ニーニョ
the U.S. National Oceanic and Atmospheric Administration: アメリカ海洋大気庁
the Intergovernmental Panel on Climate Change: 気候変動に関する政府間パネル

第1段落

[1] Coral reefs may not relate to people's daily lives, but their role in nature cannot be dismissed. They provide habitats for various types of animals and offer fishing and tourism resources. They also serve as natural embankments to protect land against big waves, including tsunami. However, the ecosystems that embrace coral reefs are under threat from the serious danger of coral bleaching — apparently due to rising sea water temperatures linked to climate change. The government and the public should realize that a key component of measures to protect coral reefs is the fight against global warming, and act accordingly.

Words 下記の語彙について、その意味を調べましょう。

	語彙	品詞	意味
1	role	名詞	
2	dismiss	動詞	
3	habitat	名詞	
4	embankment	名詞	
5	ecosystem	名詞	
6	embrace	動詞	
7	apparently	副詞	
8	temperature	名詞	
9	measure	名詞	
10	accordingly	副詞	

Phrases 下記のフレーズについて、その意味を調べましょう。

	フレーズ	意味
1	coral reefs	
2	relate to ~	
3	daily lives	
4	a role in nature	
5	various types of animals	
6	fishing resources	
7	tourism resources	
8	serve as ~	
9	protect X against Y	
10	be under threat	
11	coral bleaching	
12	due to ~	

13	be linked to ~	
14	climate change	
15	the public	
16	a key component of ~	
17	global warming	

Comprehension 本文の内容に即して、下記の質問に日本語で答えましょう。

1. 自然界におけるサンゴ礁の役割として、本文には3つのことが挙げられていますが、それらは何ですか。

2. サンゴ礁生態系が脅威にさらされている原因について、本文にはどのようなことが書かれていますか。

第2段落

[2] According to the Environment Ministry, coral reefs from the Amami Islands of Kagoshima Prefecture to the Yaeyama Islands of Okinawa Prefecture suffered large-scale bleaching last summer. In the Sekisei lagoon lying between Ishigaki Island and Iriomote Island, both in Okinawa, more than 90 percent of the coral was found bleached, and 70 percent of the coral was found to be dead. The ministry says that the current situation affecting coral in the sea off southern Japan is the most serious since large-scale bleaching in 1998. High temperatures prevailed in seawater around the world in 1997 and 1998, killing 16 percent of reef-building coral worldwide.

Words 下記の語彙について、その意味を調べましょう。

	語彙	品詞	意味
1	large-scale	形容詞	
2	lagoon	名詞	
3	bleach	動詞	
4	affect	動詞	

Unit 1　7

5	prevail	動詞	
6	seawater	名詞	
7	worldwide	副詞	

Phrases 下記のフレーズについて、その意味を調べましょう。

	フレーズ	意味
1	according to ~	
2	the Environment Ministry	
3	the Amami Islands of Kagoshima Prefecture	
4	the Yaeyama Islands of Okinawa Prefecture	
5	the current situation	
6	in the sea off southern Japan	
7	around the world	
8	reef-building coral	

Comprehension 本文の内容に即して、下記の質問に日本語で答えましょう。

1. 石西礁湖（せきせいしょうこ）で起きたこととは、どのようなことですか。

2. 1998年に起きた大規模なサンゴの白化について、本文にはどのようなことが書かれていますか。

第３段落

3 As the extensive coral damage in the late 1990s shows, bleaching of coral reefs is a global phenomenon. The Environment Ministry cites the U.S. National Oceanic and Atmospheric Administration (NOAA) as saying that El Niño events — warming of surface waters and reduced upwelling of cold, nutrient-rich water off the western coast of South America — from 2015 to 2016 have caused unprecedented widespread and long-running coral bleaching, leading to the worst damage ever in the Great Barrier Reef of Australia and Kiribati in the central Pacific Ocean. This coral bleaching mentioned by NOAA continues to this day.

Words 下記の語彙について、その意味を調べましょう。

	語彙	品詞	意味
1	extensive	形容詞	
2	cite	動詞	
3	oceanic	形容詞	
4	atmospheric	形容詞	
5	surface	名詞	
6	upwelling	名詞	
7	cause	動詞	
8	unprecedented	形容詞	
9	widespread	形容詞	
10	long-running	形容詞	
11	Kiribati	名詞	
12	mention	動詞	

Phrases 下記のフレーズについて、その意味を調べましょう。

	フレーズ	意味
1	in the late 1990s	
2	a global phenomenon	
3	nutrient-rich water	
4	off the western coast of South America	
5	lead to ~	
6	the Great Barrier Reef	
7	the central Pacific Ocean	
8	continue to this day	

Comprehension 本文の内容に即して、下記の質問に日本語で答えましょう。

1. サンゴの白化に関して NOAA が伝えていることとは、どのようなことですか。

_____
_____
_____
_____
_____

第 4 段落

4 The ministry also quotes a report by the Intergovernmental Panel on Climate Change that a rise in seawater temperature by 2 degrees Celsius can cause large-scale coral bleaching every year, inflicting devastating damage to coral reefs.

Words 下記の語彙について、その意味を調べましょう。

	語彙	品詞	意味
1	quote	動詞	
2	report	名詞	
3	intergovernmental	形容詞	
4	inflict	動詞	
5	devastating	形容詞	

Phrases 下記のフレーズについて、その意味を調べましょう。

	フレーズ	意味
1	a rise in seawater temperature	
2	2 degrees Celsius	

Comprehension 本文の内容に即して、下記の質問に日本語で答えましょう。

1. 「気候変動に関する政府間パネル」による報告書を引用して、環境省が伝えていることとは、どのようなことですか。

Writing Exercises

Phrase Writing 本文に登場するフレーズを参考にしながら、下記のフレーズを英訳しましょう。

	日本語のフレーズ	英語のフレーズ
1	様々な種類の動植物	
2	その研究によれば	
3	1980年代初頭に	
4	水温の上昇	
5	大規模な調査	

Sentence Writing 本文に登場する英文を参考にしながら、下記の和文を英訳しましょう。

1. 残念なことに、このような地球規模の現象は今日まで続いている。

2. したがって、サンゴ礁の保護につながりうる何らかの対策が必要とされる。

Vocabulary Building 下記のフレーズについて、意味が一致するものを線で結びましょう。

1. wheat flour ・　　　・ 表面張力
2. global warming ・　　　・ 大学院
3. room temperature ・　　　・ 光化学スモッグ
4. surface tension ・　　　・ 地球温暖化
5. soy sauce ・　　　・ 室温
6. photochemical smog ・　　　・ 化学調味料
7. chemical seasonings ・　　　・ 醤油
8. a graduate school ・　　　・ 小麦粉

[MEMO]

Unit 2
The Need to Protect Coral Reefs (2)

Reading Passage

5 While rising water temperatures are causing coral bleaching, it is believed that acidification of the ocean caused by higher concentration of carbon dioxide in the atmosphere may also damage coral. There is a forecast that unless stronger measures to mitigate the effects of global warming are taken, rises in seawater temperatures coupled with acidification could cause the total disappearance of coral near Japan by the 2070s.

6 In view of this serious situation, the government convened a meeting of experts in late April in Onna on Okinawa Island. The participants adopted an "emergency declaration" calling for accelerated measures to protect coral against bleaching. Proposed measures include correctly ascertaining the facts about the coral bleaching that occurred in 2016, continual and effective monitoring of the ecosystems of coral reefs with particular attention on their diversity, and sharing information on the conditions of coral reef ecosystems on a global scale through international networks such as the International Coral Reef Initiative.

7 As measures more directly related to protecting the environment in which coral lives, the experts at the meeting proposed long-term nationwide observation and forecasting the impact of rising seawater temperatures, acidification of the ocean and social and economic changes. They recommended identifying areas where healthy coral reef ecosystems can be maintained with a view to designating them as protected areas and reducing pollution there. They urged development of coral transplant and culturing technologies to revive dying coral reefs, reducing the flow of red clay, soil and sand, and polluted water into coral habitats, measures to prevent a mass generation of crowns-of-thorns starfish — a natural enemy of coral — and the promotion of ecotourism designed to educate people on coral.

8 The crucial thing that people can and need to do to protect coral is to reduce carbon dioxide emissions to prevent rises in seawater temperatures. The ability of coral to survive will increase if reefs are given time to adjust to environmental changes by reducing as much as possible increases in temperature and acidification. Japan and other countries must spare no efforts to achieve the goals set by the 2015 United Nations climate change conference in Paris: limiting rises in global temperatures from pre-industrial levels to below 2 degrees and closer to 1.5 degrees.

【369 words—*The Japan Times* (MAY 13, 2017)】

[Note] the International Coral Reef Initiative: 国際サンゴ礁イニシアティブ

第5段落

⑤ While rising water temperatures are causing coral bleaching, it is believed that acidification of the ocean caused by higher concentration of carbon dioxide in the atmosphere may also damage coral. There is a forecast that unless stronger measures to mitigate the effects of global warming are taken, rises in seawater temperatures coupled with acidification could cause the total disappearance of coral near Japan by the 2070s.

Words 下記の語彙について、その意味を調べましょう。

	語彙	品詞	意味
1	acidification	名詞	
2	concentration	名詞	
3	forecast	名詞	
4	mitigate	動詞	
5	disappearance	名詞	

Phrases 下記のフレーズについて、その意味を調べましょう。

	フレーズ	意味
1	water temperature	
2	it is believed that ---	
3	carbon dioxide	
4	in the atmosphere	
5	couple with ~	
6	by the 2070s	

Comprehension 本文の内容に即して、下記の質問に日本語で答えましょう。

1. サンゴに悪影響を及ぼすもう1つの原因として、本文にはどのようなことが挙げられていますか。

2. 2070年代までに起こる事柄として、本文ではどのような予測がなされていますか。

6 In view of this serious situation, the government convened a meeting of experts in late April in Onna on Okinawa Island. The participants adopted an "emergency declaration" calling for accelerated measures to protect coral against bleaching. Proposed measures include correctly ascertaining the facts about the coral bleaching that occurred in 2016, continual and effective monitoring of the ecosystems of coral reefs with particular attention on their diversity, and sharing information on the conditions of coral reef ecosystems on a global scale through international networks such as the International Coral Reef Initiative.

Words 下記の語彙について、その意味を調べましょう。

	語彙	品詞	意味
1	convene	動詞	
2	expert	名詞	
3	participant	名詞	
4	adopt	動詞	
5	accelerated	形容詞	
6	correctly	副詞	
7	ascertain	動詞	
8	continual	形容詞	
9	effective	形容詞	
10	monitor	動詞	
11	diversity	名詞	
12	share	動詞	

Phrases 下記のフレーズについて、その意味を調べましょう。

	フレーズ	意味
1	in view of ~	
2	in late April	
3	an emergency declaration	
4	call for ~	
5	with particular attention on ~	
6	on a global scale	

Comprehension 本文の内容に即して、下記の質問に日本語で答えましょう。

1. 政府主催の専門家会議で提案された対策として、本文では3つのことが述べられていますが、その3つのこととはどのようなことですか。

___

___

___

第 7 段落

[7] As measures more directly related to protecting the environment in which coral lives, the experts at the meeting proposed long-term nationwide observation and forecasting the impact of rising seawater temperatures, acidification of the ocean and social and economic changes. They recommended identifying areas where healthy coral reef ecosystems can be maintained with a view to designating them as protected areas and reducing pollution there. They urged development of coral transplant and culturing technologies to revive dying coral reefs, reducing the flow of red clay, soil and sand, and polluted water into coral habitats, measures to prevent a mass generation of crowns-of-thorns starfish — a natural enemy of coral — and the promotion of ecotourism designed to educate people on coral.

Words 下記の語彙について、その意味を調べましょう。

	語彙	品詞	意味
1	long-term	形容詞	
2	nationwide	形容詞	
3	observation	名詞	
4	forecast	動詞	
5	impact	名詞	
6	recommend	動詞	
7	identify	動詞	
8	maintain	動詞	
9	designate	動詞	
10	pollution	名詞	
11	urge	動詞	
12	revive	動詞	
13	soil	名詞	
14	sand	名詞	
15	mass	形容詞	

| 16 | promotion | 名詞 | |
| 17 | ecotourism | 名詞 | |

Phrases 下記のフレーズについて、その意味を調べましょう。

	フレーズ	意味
1	be related to ~	
2	with a view to *doing*	
3	protected areas	
4	transplant technologies	
5	culturing technologies	
6	the flow of X into Y	
7	red clay	
8	polluted water	
9	a mass generation	
10	crowns-of-thorns starfish	
11	a natural enemy	
12	be designed to *do*	
13	educate people on coral	

Comprehension 本文の内容に即して、下記の質問に日本語で答えましょう。

1. 政府主催の専門家会議で提案ないし推奨されたさらなる対策として、本文では6つのことが述べられていますが、その6つのこととはどのようなことですか。

第 8 段落

[8] The crucial thing that people can and need to do to protect coral is to reduce carbon dioxide emissions to prevent rises in seawater temperatures. The ability of coral to survive will increase if reefs are given time to adjust to environmental changes by reducing as much as possible increases in temperature and acidification. Japan and other countries must spare no efforts to achieve the goals set by the 2015 United

Nations climate change conference in Paris: limiting rises in global temperatures from pre-industrial levels to below 2 degrees and closer to 1.5 degrees.

Words 下記の語彙について、その意味を調べましょう。

	語彙	品詞	意味
1	crucial	形容詞	
2	conference	名詞	
3	pre-industrial	形容詞	
4	degree	名詞	

Phrases 下記のフレーズについて、その意味を調べましょう。

	フレーズ	意味
1	carbon dioxide emissions	
2	adjust to ~	
3	environmental changes	
4	as much as possible	
5	spare no efforts to *do*	
6	achieve the goals	
7	the United Nations	
8	limit X to Y	
9	rises in global temperatures	
10	be close to ~	

Comprehension 本文の内容に即して、下記の質問に日本語で答えましょう。

1. サンゴを守るために私たちができることとは、どのようなことですか。

2. 2015年にパリで開催された国連気候変動会議で定められた目標とは、どのような目標ですか。

Writing Exercises

Phrase Writing
本文に登場するフレーズを参考にしながら、下記のフレーズを英訳しましょう。

	日本語のフレーズ	英語のフレーズ
1	9月初頭に	
2	大気中の酸素	
3	長期記憶	
4	汚染水の処理	
5	社会変化に適応する	

Sentence Writing
本文に登場する英文を参考にしながら、下記の和文を英訳しましょう。

1. この深刻な状況は、地球規模で解決する必要がある。

2. 私たちにできる唯一のことは、サンゴ礁生態系に関する情報を共有することである。

Vocabulary Building
下記のフレーズについて、意味が一致するものを線で結びましょう。

1. large-scale agriculture ・　・乳製品
2. dairy products ・　・理論物理学
3. a positive reaction ・　・高血圧
4. mass production ・　・食中毒
5. high blood pressure ・　・陽性反応
6. population density ・　・大規模農業
7. food poisoning ・　・大量生産
8. theoretical physics ・　・人口密度

[MEMO]

Unit 3
AlphaGo AI Stuns Go Community (1)

Reading Passage

[1] Google's artificial intelligence program AlphaGo stunned players and fans of the ancient Chinese board game of go last year by defeating South Korean grandmaster Lee Sedol 4-1. Last month, an upgraded version of the program achieved a more astonishing feat by trouncing Ke Jie from China, the world's top player, 3-0 in a five-game contest. In the world of go, AI appears to have surpassed humans, ushering in an age in which human players will need to learn from AI. What happened in the game of go also poses a larger question of how humans can coexist with AI in other fields.

[2] In a go match, two players alternately lay black and white stones on 361 points of intersection on a board with a 19-by-19 grid of lines, trying to seal off a larger territory than the opponent. It is said that the number of possible moves amounts to 10 to the power of 360. This huge variety of options compels even top-class players to differ on the question of which moves are the best. Such freedom to maneuver caused experts to believe it would take a while before AI would catch up with humans in the world of go. Against this background, AlphaGo's sweeping victory over the world's No. 1 player is a significant event that not only symbolizes the rapid development of computer science but is also encouraging for the application of AI in various fields.

[3] In part of the contest with Lee in Seoul in March 2016, AlphaGo made irrational moves, cornering itself into a disadvantageous position. But in the case of its contest with Ke in the eastern Chinese city of Wuzhen in late May, it made convincing moves throughout, subjecting the human to a "horrible experience." He called AlphaGo "a go player like a god."

[4] AlphaGo was built by DeepMind, a Google subsidiary. It takes advantage of technology known as deep learning, which utilizes neural networks similar to those of human brains to learn from a vast amount of data and enhance judging power. This is analogous to a baby learning a language by being exposed to a huge volume of utterances over a period of time. The program not only learns effective patterns of moves for go by studying enormous volumes of documented previous games but also hones its skills by playing millions of games against itself. In this manner, it has accomplished a remarkable evolution over the past year. Unlike humans, it is free of fatigue and emotional fluctuations. Because it grows stronger by playing games against itself, there is no knowing how good it will become in the future.

【437 words—*The Japan Times* (JUN 3, 2017)】

[Notes] Lee Sedol: 李世乭（イ・セドル）氏　Ke Jie: 柯潔（カー・ジエ）氏　Wuzhen: 烏鎮（ウーチン）
DeepMind: ディープマインド（企業名）

第 1 段落

1. Google's artificial intelligence program AlphaGo stunned players and fans of the ancient Chinese board game of go last year by defeating South Korean grandmaster Lee Sedol 4-1. Last month, an upgraded version of the program achieved a more astonishing feat by trouncing Ke Jie from China, the world's top player, 3-0 in a five-game contest. In the world of go, AI appears to have surpassed humans, ushering in an age in which human players will need to learn from AI. What happened in the game of go also poses a larger question of how humans can coexist with AI in other fields.

Words 下記の語彙について、その意味を調べましょう。

	語彙	品詞	意味
1	stun	動詞	
2	ancient	形容詞	
3	defeat	動詞	
4	grandmaster	名詞	
5	astonishing	形容詞	
6	feat	名詞	
7	trounce	動詞	
8	surpass	動詞	
9	age	名詞	
10	pose	動詞	

Phrases 下記のフレーズについて、その意味を調べましょう。

	フレーズ	意味
1	artificial intelligence	
2	a board game	
3	an upgraded version	
4	a five-game contest	
5	usher in ~	
6	coexist with ~	
7	in other fields	

Comprehension 本文の内容に即して、下記の質問に日本語で答えましょう。

1. 「アルファ碁」が驚異的であることを裏づける事実として、本文には2つのことが書かれていますが、その2つのこととはどのようなことですか。

2. 囲碁の世界で起こったことが私たちに投げかけていることとは、どのようなことですか。

第 2 段落

2 In a go match, two players alternately lay black and white stones on 361 points of intersection on a board with a 19-by-19 grid of lines, trying to seal off a larger territory than the opponent. It is said that the number of possible moves amounts to 10 to the power of 360. This huge variety of options compels even top-class players to differ on the question of which moves are the best. Such freedom to maneuver caused experts to believe it would take a while before AI would catch up with humans in the world of go. Against this background, AlphaGo's sweeping victory over the world's No. 1 player is a significant event that not only symbolizes the rapid development of computer science but is also encouraging for the application of AI in various fields.

Words 下記の語彙について、その意味を調べましょう。

	語彙	品詞	意味
1	alternately	副詞	
2	territory	名詞	
3	opponent	名詞	
4	huge	形容詞	
5	option	名詞	
6	freedom	名詞	
7	maneuver	動詞	
8	expert	名詞	
9	significant	形容詞	
10	symbolize	動詞	

11	rapid	形容詞	
12	encouraging	形容詞	
13	application	名詞	

Phrases 下記のフレーズについて、その意味を調べましょう。

	フレーズ	意味
1	a point of intersection	
2	a 19-by-19 grid of lines	
3	seal off ~	
4	it is said that ---	
5	amount to ~	
6	10 to the power of 360	
7	compel X to *do*	
8	cause X to *do*	
9	take a while	
10	catch up with ~	
11	against this background	
12	a sweeping victory	
13	a victory over ~	
14	computer science	
15	in various fields	

Comprehension 本文の内容に即して、下記の質問に日本語で答えましょう。

1. トップ囲碁棋士を悩ませている問題として、本文にはどのようなことが書かれていますか。

2. アルファ碁の圧勝によってもたらされる帰結として、本文にはどのようなことが書かれていますか。

第3段落

3 In part of the contest with Lee in Seoul in March 2016, AlphaGo made irrational moves, cornering itself into a disadvantageous position. But in the case of its contest with Ke in the eastern Chinese city of Wuzhen in late May, it made convincing moves throughout, subjecting the human to a "horrible experience." He called AlphaGo "a go player like a god."

Words 下記の語彙について、その意味を調べましょう。

	語彙	品詞	意味
1	irrational	形容詞	
2	disadvantageous	形容詞	
3	eastern	形容詞	
4	convincing	形容詞	
5	throughout	副詞	
6	horrible	形容詞	
7	experience	名詞	

Phrases 下記のフレーズについて、その意味を調べましょう。

	フレーズ	意味
1	part of ~	
2	corner X into Y	
3	in the case of ~	
4	in late May	
5	subject X to Y	

Comprehension 本文の内容に即して、下記の質問に日本語で答えましょう。

1. 2016年3月にソウルで行われた李（イ）氏との対局で、アルファ碁に生じたこととは、どのようなことですか。

2. 柯（カー）氏は、アルファ碁について、どのような評価を下していますか。

第 4 段落

4 AlphaGo was built by DeepMind, a Google subsidiary. It takes advantage of technology known as deep learning, which utilizes neural networks similar to those of human brains to learn from a vast amount of data and enhance judging power. This is analogous to a baby learning a language by being exposed to a huge volume of utterances over a period of time. The program not only learns effective patterns of moves for go by studying enormous volumes of documented previous games but also hones its skills by playing millions of games against itself. In this manner, it has accomplished a remarkable evolution over the past year. Unlike humans, it is free of fatigue and emotional fluctuations. Because it grows stronger by playing games against itself, there is no knowing how good it will become in the future.

Words 下記の語彙について、その意味を調べましょう。

	語彙	品詞	意味
1	subsidiary	名詞	
2	utilize	動詞	
3	enhance	動詞	
4	utterance	名詞	
5	effective	形容詞	
6	document	動詞	
7	previous	形容詞	
8	accomplish	動詞	
9	remarkable	形容詞	
10	evolution	名詞	
11	fatigue	名詞	
12	fluctuation	名詞	

Phrases 下記のフレーズについて、その意味を調べましょう。

	フレーズ	意味
1	take advantage of ~	
2	be known as ~	
3	deep learning	
4	neural networks	
5	a vast amount of data	
6	judging power	
7	be analogous to ~	
8	be exposed to ~	

9	a huge volume of utterances	
10	over a period of time	
11	enormous volumes of games	
12	hone its skills	
13	millions of games	
14	in this manner	
15	over the past year	
16	unlike humans	
17	be free of ~	
18	emotional fluctuations	
19	there is no knowing	
20	in the future	

Comprehension　本文の内容に即して、下記の質問に日本語で答えましょう。

1. アルファ碁の開発において、DeepMind（ディープマインド）という企業が利用した技術とは、どのような技術のことですか。

2. アルファ碁の学習技術について、本文にはどのようなことが書かれていますか。

Writing Exercises

Phrase Writing 本文に登場するフレーズを参考にしながら、下記のフレーズを英訳しましょう。

	日本語のフレーズ	英語のフレーズ
1	修正版	
2	7の25乗	
3	環境科学	
4	後者の場合には	
5	近い将来	

Sentence Writing 本文に登場する英文を参考にしながら、下記の和文を英訳しましょう。

1. この五番勝負の対局は、9月下旬に日本で行われた。

2. 囲碁の世界で起きたことは、人工知能の急速な発展を象徴している。

Vocabulary Building 下記のフレーズについて、意味が一致するものを線で結びましょう。

1. overfishing   ・ ・老廃物
2. the ozone layer   ・ ・ペットボトル
3. waste matter   ・ ・オゾン層
4. agricultural water ・ ・魚の乱獲
5. marine pollution   ・ ・原料
6. raw materials   ・ ・農業用水
7. a plastic bottle   ・ ・肺がん
8. lung cancer   ・ ・海洋汚染

Unit 4
AlphaGo AI Stuns Go Community (2)

Reading Passage

5 Feeling intimidated by AI programs should not be the only reaction of human go players. They can receive inspiration from AlphaGo since it shows a superior grasp of the whole situation of a contest, instead of being obsessed with localized moves, and it often lays stones in and around the center of the board. Human players usually first try to seal off territory around the corners. Its playing records also prove that even some moves traditionally considered as bad have advantages. By learning from AlphaGo, go players can acquire new skills and make their contests more interesting.

6 AlphaGo does have a weak point. It cannot explain its thinking behind the particular moves that it makes. When watching ordinary go contests, fans can enjoy listening to analyses by professional players. Also, ordinary go contests are interesting since psychology plays such an important part of the game, especially at critical points. This shows there are some elements of go that AI cannot take over.

7 DeepMind is thinking about how it can apply the know-how it has accumulated through the AlphaGo program to other areas, such as developing drugs and diagnosing patients through data analysis. But the fact that the program made irrational moves during its match with South Korea's Lee shows that the technology is not error-free — a problem that must be resolved before AI can be applied to such fields as medical services and self-driving vehicles. Many problems may have to be overcome to make AI safe enough for application in areas where human lives are at stake.

8 A report issued by Nomura Research Institute says that in 10 to 20 years, AI may be capable of taking over jobs now being done by 49 percent of Japan's workforce. At the same time, it says AI cannot intrude into fields where cooperation or harmony between people is needed or where people create abstract concepts like art, historical studies, philosophy and theology. It will be all the more important for both the public and private sectors to make serious efforts to cultivate people's ability to think and create while finding out what proper roles AI should play in society.

【357 words—*The Japan Times* (JUN 3, 2017)】

[Notes] Nomura Research Institute: 野村総合研究所（野村総研）
DeepMind: ディープマインド（企業名）

第 5 段落

5 Feeling intimidated by AI programs should not be the only reaction of human go players. They can receive inspiration from AlphaGo since it shows a superior grasp of the whole situation of a contest, instead of being obsessed with localized moves, and it often lays stones in and around the center of the board. Human players usually first try to seal off territory around the corners. Its playing records also prove that even some moves traditionally considered as bad have advantages. By learning from AlphaGo, go players can acquire new skills and make their contests more interesting.

Words 下記の語彙について、その意味を調べましょう。

	語彙	品詞	意味
1	intimidate	動詞	
2	inspiration	名詞	
3	superior	形容詞	
4	grasp	名詞	
5	localize	動詞	
6	prove	動詞	
7	traditionally	副詞	
8	advantage	名詞	
9	acquire	動詞	

Phrases 下記のフレーズについて、その意味を調べましょう。

	フレーズ	意味
1	the only reaction	
2	be obsessed with ~	
3	its playing records	
4	be considered as bad	

Comprehension 本文の内容に即して、下記の質問に日本語で答えましょう。

1. アルファ碁から囲碁の技術を学ぶことが可能であると考えられるのは、なぜですか。

第 **6** 段落

[6] AlphaGo does have a weak point. It cannot explain its thinking behind the particular moves that it makes. When watching ordinary go contests, fans can enjoy listening to analyses by professional players. Also, ordinary go contests are interesting since psychology plays such an important part of the game, especially at critical points. This shows there are some elements of go that AI cannot take over.

Words 下記の語彙について、その意味を調べましょう。

	語彙	品詞	意味
1	explain	動詞	
2	thinking	名詞	
3	ordinary	形容詞	
4	analysis / analyses	名詞	
5	psychology	名詞	
6	especially	副詞	
7	element	名詞	

Phrases 下記のフレーズについて、その意味を調べましょう。

	フレーズ	意味
1	have a weak point	
2	at critical points	
3	take over	

Comprehension 本文の内容に即して、下記の質問に日本語で答えましょう。

1. アルファ碁の弱点として、本文ではどのようなことが指摘されていますか。

第 7 段落

7 DeepMind is thinking about how it can apply the know-how it has accumulated through the AlphaGo program to other areas, such as developing drugs and diagnosing patients through data analysis. But the fact that the program made irrational moves during its match with South Korea's Lee shows that the technology is not error-free — a problem that must be resolved before AI can be applied to such fields as medical services and self-driving vehicles. Many problems may have to be overcome to make AI safe enough for application in areas where human lives are at stake.

Words 下記の語彙について、その意味を調べましょう。

	語彙	品詞	意味
1	know-how	名詞	
2	accumulate	動詞	
3	diagnose	動詞	
4	overcome	動詞	

Phrases 下記のフレーズについて、その意味を調べましょう。

	フレーズ	意味
1	apply X to Y	
2	develop drugs	
3	through data analysis	
4	be error-free	
5	medical services	
6	self-driving vehicles	
7	human lives	
8	be at stake	

Comprehension 本文の内容に即して、下記の質問に日本語で答えましょう。

1. DeepMind（ディープマインド）は、アルファ碁で蓄積してきたノウハウを、どのような分野に応用していきたいと考えていますか。

2. 韓国の李（イ）氏との対局中に、プログラムが理解に苦しむ打ち手をしてしまったことは、人工知能について、どのようなことを示唆していますか。

第8段落

⑧ A report issued by Nomura Research Institute says that in 10 to 20 years, AI may be capable of taking over jobs now being done by 49 percent of Japan's workforce. At the same time, it says AI cannot intrude into fields where cooperation or harmony between people is needed or where people create abstract concepts like art, historical studies, philosophy and theology. It will be all the more important for both the public and private sectors to make serious efforts to cultivate people's ability to think and create while finding out what proper roles AI should play in society.

Words 下記の語彙について、その意味を調べましょう。

	語彙	品詞	意味
1	report	名詞	
2	issue	動詞	
3	workforce	名詞	
4	cooperation	名詞	
5	harmony	名詞	
6	philosophy	名詞	
7	theology	名詞	
8	cultivate	動詞	
9	proper	形容詞	
10	role	名詞	

Phrases 下記のフレーズについて、その意味を調べましょう。

	フレーズ	意味
1	in 10 to 20 years	
2	be capable of *doing*	
3	take over jobs	
4	at the same time	

5	intrude into ~	
6	abstract concepts	
7	historical studies	
8	all the more	
9	the public	
10	private sectors	
11	make serious efforts	

Comprehension 本文の内容に即して、下記の質問に日本語で答えましょう。

1. 野村総研によって発行された報告書には、人工知能に関して、2つのことが述べられていると本文には書かれていますが、その2つのこととは、どのようなことですか。

[MEMO]

Writing Exercises

Phrase Writing
本文に登場するフレーズを参考にしながら、下記のフレーズを英訳しましょう。

	日本語のフレーズ	英語のフレーズ
1	唯一の利点	
2	弱点は何もない	
3	具体概念	
4	遺伝研究	
5	これらの問題を克服する	

Sentence Writing
本文に登場する英文を参考にしながら、下記の和文を英訳しましょう。

1. この技術を他の領域に応用することは、かなり難しいかもしれない。

2. 社会の中で人工知能が果たすべきいくつかの役割について、次に検討してみよう。

Vocabulary Building
下記のフレーズについて、意味が一致するものを線で結びましょう。

1. harmful substances ・　・ 分子生物学
2. sesame oil ・　・ 環境権
3. experimental data ・　・ 有害物質
4. environmental rights ・　・ ゴマ油
5. molecular biology ・　・ 原油
6. natural disasters ・　・ 遺伝子組換え作物
7. crude oil ・　・ 自然災害
8. genetically modified crops ・　・ 実験データ

[MEMO]

Unit 5
Safe Driving by Senior Citizens (1)

Reading Passage

1 A recent series of fatal accidents involving cars driven by elderly people has led the government to organize an urgent meeting of officials in which Prime Minister Shinzo Abe told his Cabinet ministers to tackle the problem. Both the national and local governments should take concrete steps to prevent such accidents, including by properly assessing the driving ability of senior citizens while working out measures to secure alternate means of transport for elderly residents — particularly in rural areas where public transportation services have become meager.

2 What is tragic and dreadful about these accidents is that people's everyday tools suddenly turn into lethal instruments. In October, an 83-year-old man slammed his light truck into a group of schoolchildren on a walkway in Yokohama after he lost control of the vehicle, killing a first-grader and injuring four other pupils.

3 Although evidence indicates the man had been driving in Tokyo and Kanagawa Prefecture since the day before, he told the police he didn't remember where he had been and had almost no recall of what he was doing before the fatal crash.

4 The police suspect he suffers from senile dementia. No irregularities were found in a cognitive function test when he last renewed his driver's license, but that was three years ago.

5 The Yokohama case was followed by two fatal accidents involving drivers in their 80s earlier this month. In Shimotsuke, Tochigi Prefecture, an 84-year-old man crashed his car into an entrance to a hospital, killing one pedestrian and injuring two others.

6 Two days later, a car driven by an 83-year-old woman struck and killed two people on a sidewalk in the compounds of a hospital in western Tokyo, with the driver herself suffering serious injuries. The accident occurred on her way home from visiting her husband at the hospital — she said she started driving that car in September to see the husband there. The police suspect the woman — who held a "gold" driver's license because she had a perfect driving record — mistook the gas pedal for the brake pedal.

【337 words—*The Japan Times* (NOV 26, 2016)】

第 1 段落

1 A recent series of fatal accidents involving cars driven by elderly people has led the government to organize an urgent meeting of officials in which Prime Minister Shinzo Abe told his Cabinet ministers to tackle the problem. Both the national and local governments should take concrete steps to prevent such accidents, including by properly assessing the driving ability of senior citizens while working out measures to secure alternate means of transport for elderly residents — particularly in rural areas where public transportation services have become meager.

Words 下記の語彙について、その意味を調べましょう。

	語彙	品詞	意味
1	involve	動詞	
2	elderly	形容詞	
3	organize	動詞	
4	urgent	形容詞	
5	official	名詞	
6	tackle	動詞	
7	concrete	形容詞	
8	properly	副詞	
9	assess	動詞	
10	measure	名詞	
11	secure	動詞	
12	alternate	形容詞	
13	resident	名詞	
14	particularly	副詞	
15	meager	形容詞	

Phrases 下記のフレーズについて、その意味を調べましょう。

	フレーズ	意味
1	a series of ~	
2	fatal accidents	
3	elderly people	
4	lead X to *do*	
5	Prime Minister	
6	a Cabinet minister	
7	the national government	
8	the local governments	

9	take concrete steps to *do*	
10	senior citizens	
11	work out	
12	(a) means of transport	
13	in rural areas	
14	public transportation services	

Comprehension 本文の内容に即して、下記の質問に日本語で答えましょう。

1. 本文では、高齢者の交通事故を防止するために、政府はどのような対策をとるべきだと主張していますか。

___

___

___

___

___

第2段落

2 What is tragic and dreadful about these accidents is that people's everyday tools suddenly turn into lethal instruments. In October, an 83-year-old man slammed his light truck into a group of schoolchildren on a walkway in Yokohama after he lost control of the vehicle, killing a first-grader and injuring four other pupils.

Words 下記の語彙について、その意味を調べましょう。

	語彙	品詞	意味
1	tragic	形容詞	
2	dreadful	形容詞	
3	everyday	形容詞	
4	suddenly	副詞	
5	lethal	形容詞	
6	walkway	名詞	
7	vehicle	名詞	
8	injure	動詞	
9	pupil	名詞	

Phrases 下記のフレーズについて、その意味を調べましょう。

	フレーズ	意味
1	turn into ~	
2	a lethal instrument	
3	slam X into Y	
4	a light truck	
5	lose control of ~	
6	a first-grader	

Comprehension 本文の内容に即して、下記の質問に日本語で答えましょう。

1. 10月に横浜で起きた事故とは、どのような事故ですか。

_____
_____
_____
_____

第 3 段落

[3] Although evidence indicates the man had been driving in Tokyo and Kanagawa Prefecture since the day before, he told the police he didn't remember where he had been and had almost no recall of what he was doing before the fatal crash.

Words 下記の語彙について、その意味を調べましょう。

	語彙	品詞	意味
1	evidence	名詞	
2	indicate	動詞	
3	prefecture	名詞	
4	crash	名詞	

Phrases 下記のフレーズについて、その意味を調べましょう。

	フレーズ	意味
1	the day before	
2	almost no	
3	have no recall of ~	

Comprehension 本文の内容に即して、下記の質問に日本語で答えましょう。

1. 横浜で交通死亡事故を起こした 80 代の男性は、警察にどのようなことを供述していますか。

_____
_____
_____
_____

第 4 段落

④ The police suspect he suffers from senile dementia. No irregularities were found in a cognitive function test when he last renewed his driver's license, but that was three years ago.

Words 下記の語彙について、その意味を調べましょう。

	語彙	品詞	意味
1	suspect	動詞	
2	irregularity	名詞	
3	renew	動詞	

Phrases 下記のフレーズについて、その意味を調べましょう。

	フレーズ	意味
1	suffer from ~	
2	senile dementia	
3	a cognitive function test	
4	a driver's license	

Comprehension 本文の内容に即して、下記の質問に日本語で答えましょう。

1. 警察は、事故を起こした男性に対して、どのようなことを疑っていますか。

_____
_____
_____
_____
_____

第5段落

[5] The Yokohama case was followed by two fatal accidents involving drivers in their 80s earlier this month. In Shimotsuke, Tochigi Prefecture, an 84-year-old man crashed his car into an entrance to a hospital, killing one pedestrian and injuring two others.

Words 下記の語彙について、その意味を調べましょう。

	語彙	品詞	意味
1	entrance	名詞	
2	pedestrian	名詞	

Phrases 下記のフレーズについて、その意味を調べましょう。

	フレーズ	意味
1	X is followed by Y	
2	drivers in their 80s	
3	earlier this month	
4	crash X into Y	

Comprehension 本文の内容に即して、下記の質問に日本語で答えましょう。

1. 横浜での事故に続き、栃木県ではどのような事故が起こりましたか。

___

第6段落

[6] Two days later, a car driven by an 83-year-old woman struck and killed two people on a sidewalk in the compounds of a hospital in western Tokyo, with the driver herself suffering serious injuries. The accident occurred on her way home from visiting her husband at the hospital — she said she started driving that car in September to see the husband there. The police suspect the woman — who held a "gold" driver's license because she had a perfect driving record — mistook the gas pedal for the brake pedal.

Words 下記の語彙について、その意味を調べましょう。

	語彙	品詞	意味
1	strike	動詞	
2	sidewalk	名詞	
3	compound	名詞	

Phrases 下記のフレーズについて、その意味を調べましょう。

	フレーズ	意味
1	two days later	
2	in western Tokyo	
3	serious injuries	
4	on *one's* way home from ~	
5	start *doing*	
6	hold a "gold" driver's license	
7	have a perfect driving record	
8	mistake X for Y	
9	a gas pedal	
10	a brake pedal	

Comprehension 本文の内容に即して、下記の質問に日本語で答えましょう。

1. 西東京で83歳の女性が起こした事故は、どのようなことが原因だったと、地元警察は考えていますか。

___

___

___

___

___

Unit 5 43

Writing Exercises

Phrase Writing
本文に登場するフレーズを参考にしながら、下記のフレーズを英訳しましょう。

	日本語のフレーズ	英語のフレーズ
1	一連の新聞記事	
2	意思疎通のための代替手段	
3	高校生の一団	
4	17歳の学生	
5	仕事から帰る途中で	

Sentence Writing
本文に登場する英文を参考にしながら、下記の和文を英訳しましょう。

1. 愛知県と長野県は、その問題のすべてに取り組むべきである。

2. 彼女がアクセルとブレーキを踏み間違えたことを示す証拠は何もない。

Vocabulary Building
下記のフレーズについて、意味が一致するものを線で結びましょう。

1. a poisonous spider   ・   ・粉砂糖
2. a tree diagram   ・   ・緑茶
3. green tea   ・   ・嗅覚
4. sweet potatoes   ・   ・毒グモ
5. powdered sugar   ・   ・樹形図
6. the sense of smell   ・   ・華道
7. skin cells   ・   ・サツマイモ
8. flower arrangement   ・   ・皮膚細胞

Unit 6
Safe Driving by Senior Citizens (2)

Reading Passage

[7] According to the National Police Agency, 4.36 fatal traffic accidents occurred per 100,000 drivers last year. The figure goes up with the age of drivers — 6.99 for those aged 75 to 79; 11.53 for those from 80 to 84 and 18.17 among drivers 85 and older. As of the end of 2015, some 4.78 million licensed drivers were 75 and older — an increase of 300,000, or 6.8 percent, from a year earlier. The number of elderly drivers is expected to rise as the graying of the nation's population progresses.

[8] Other NPA statistics are also revealing. In 26 percent of the some 3,600 fatal traffic accidents in 2014, drivers 65 and above committed gross negligence — an increase of nearly 10 points over the past decade. According to the transport ministry, 69 percent of the 739 drivers who drove their vehicles the wrong way on expressways from 2011 to 2014 were 65 and older — with 9 percent of them suspected of suffering from senile dementia.

[9] Beginning in March, an amendment to the Road Traffic Law will require a stricter cognitive function test for drivers 75 and older when they renew their licenses every three years. If the drivers show signs of deficiency in memory and judgment, they must see a doctor, and if they are diagnosed with dementia, their licenses will be either revoked or suspended. If elderly drivers violate traffic rules, they will be required to take an extra cognitive function test.

[10] The NPA has for years been calling on elderly drivers who have lost confidence in their driving skills to voluntarily return their licenses. Last year, 123,913 drivers aged 75 and older did so, accounting for about 43 percent of the senior citizens who took this step.

[11] The government should consider whether the steps taken are enough to prevent accidents involving senior drivers. It should also think about increasing the frequency of cognitive functions testing to detect early signs of dementia. Another important step is taking into account other factors linked to advanced age that affect people's ability to drive — such as declining eyesight and slower response times. The introduction of additional tests to gauge elderly drivers' physical abilities should also be considered.

[12] Such steps should go hand in hand with measures to secure convenient daily transportation options for senior citizens who have to give up driving. These should include the distribution of discount coupons for buses and taxis, and the introduction of more low-cost public transport. Such measures will be strongly needed in rural depopulated areas where public transportation services such as buses are being cut back. Communities must strive to ensure that the transportation needs of local elderly residents who no longer drive can be met. 【449 words—*The Japan Times* (NOV 26, 2016)】

第 7 段落

7 According to the National Police Agency, 4.36 fatal traffic accidents occurred per 100,000 drivers last year. The figure goes up with the age of drivers — 6.99 for those aged 75 to 79; 11.53 for those from 80 to 84 and 18.17 among drivers 85 and older. As of the end of 2015, some 4.78 million licensed drivers were 75 and older — an increase of 300,000, or 6.8 percent, from a year earlier. The number of elderly drivers is expected to rise as the graying of the nation's population progresses.

Words 下記の語彙について、その意味を調べましょう。

	語彙	品詞	意味
1	figure	名詞	
2	some	形容詞	
3	million	名詞	
4	graying	名詞	
5	population	名詞	
6	progress	動詞	

Phrases 下記のフレーズについて、その意味を調べましょう。

	フレーズ	意味
1	according to ~	
2	the National Police Agency	
3	fatal traffic accidents	
4	per 100,000 drivers	
5	go up	
6	those aged 75 to 79	
7	as of the end of 2015	
8	licensed drivers	
9	a year earlier	
10	the number of elderly drivers	
11	be expected to *do*	

Comprehension 本文の内容に即して、下記の質問に日本語で答えましょう。

1. 警察庁は、昨年起こった交通死亡事故に関して、どのようなことを発表していますか。

2. 高齢の運転手が今後増加すると考えられるのは、なぜですか。

第 8 段落

8 Other NPA statistics are also revealing. In 26 percent of the some 3,600 fatal traffic accidents in 2014, drivers 65 and above committed gross negligence — an increase of nearly 10 points over the past decade. According to the transport ministry, 69 percent of the 739 drivers who drove their vehicles the wrong way on expressways from 2011 to 2014 were 65 and older — with 9 percent of them suspected of suffering from senile dementia.

Words 下記の語彙について、その意味を調べましょう。

	語彙	品詞	意味
1	statistics	名詞	
2	reveal	動詞	
3	commit	動詞	
4	nearly	副詞	
5	transport	名詞	
6	expressway	名詞	

Phrases 下記のフレーズについて、その意味を調べましょう。

	フレーズ	意味
1	gross negligence	
2	over the past decade	
3	the transport ministry	
4	be suspected of ~	

Comprehension 本文の内容に即して、下記の質問に日本語で答えましょう。

1. 警察庁の別の統計では、どのようなことが明らかになっていますか。

2. 国土交通省の統計では、高齢の運転手に関して、どのようなことが明らかになっていますか。

第 9 段落

⑨ Beginning in March, an amendment to the Road Traffic Law will require a stricter cognitive function test for drivers 75 and older when they renew their licenses every three years. If the drivers show signs of deficiency in memory and judgment, they must see a doctor, and if they are diagnosed with dementia, their licenses will be either revoked or suspended. If elderly drivers violate traffic rules, they will be required to take an extra cognitive function test.

Words 下記の語彙について、その意味を調べましょう。

	語彙	品詞	意味
1	strict	形容詞	
2	judgment	名詞	
3	revoke	動詞	
4	suspend	動詞	
5	violate	動詞	
6	extra	形容詞	

Phrases 下記のフレーズについて、その意味を調べましょう。

	フレーズ	意味
1	an amendment to ~	
2	the Road Traffic Law	
3	every three years	
4	a sign of deficiency	
5	deficiency in memory and judgment	
6	see a doctor	
7	be diagnosed with ~	
8	traffic rules	
9	be required to *do*	
10	take a test	

Comprehension　本文の内容に即して、下記の質問に日本語で答えましょう。

1. 道路交通法の改正により、75歳以上の運転手には、どのような義務が課されるようになりましたか。

   _____
   _____
   _____
   _____

2. 認知機能検査で、運転手が認知症と診断された場合、どのような措置が取られることになりますか。

   _____
   _____
   _____
   _____

第10段落

10　The NPA has for years been calling on elderly drivers who have lost confidence in their driving skills to voluntarily return their licenses. Last year, 123,913 drivers aged 75 and older did so, accounting for about 43 percent of the senior citizens who took this step.

Words　下記の語彙について、その意味を調べましょう。

	語彙	品詞	意味
1	voluntarily	副詞	

Phrases　下記のフレーズについて、その意味を調べましょう。

	フレーズ	意味
1	for years	
2	call on X to *do*	
3	lose confidence in ~	
4	driving skills	
5	account for ~	

Comprehension 本文の内容に即して、下記の質問に日本語で答えましょう。

1. ここ数年、警察庁は、高齢の運転手にどのようなことを呼びかけてきましたか。

第11段落

11 The government should consider whether the steps taken are enough to prevent accidents involving senior drivers. It should also think about increasing the frequency of cognitive functions testing to detect early signs of dementia. Another important step is taking into account other factors linked to advanced age that affect people's ability to drive — such as declining eyesight and slower response times. The introduction of additional tests to gauge elderly drivers' physical abilities should also be considered.

Words 下記の語彙について、その意味を調べましょう。

	語彙	品詞	意味
1	consider	動詞	
2	prevent	動詞	
3	frequency	名詞	
4	testing	名詞	
5	detect	動詞	
6	factor	名詞	
7	affect	動詞	
8	decline	動詞	
9	eyesight	名詞	
10	response	名詞	
11	introduction	名詞	
12	additional	形容詞	
13	gauge	動詞	

Phrases 下記のフレーズについて、その意味を調べましょう。

	フレーズ	意味
1	be enough to *do*	
2	early signs of ~	
3	take ~ into account	
4	be linked to ~	
5	advanced age	
6	response times	
7	physical abilities	

Comprehension 本文の内容に即して、下記の質問に日本語で答えましょう。

1. 本文では、高齢の運転手による事故を防ぐために、3つのことが提案されていますが、それらはどのようなことですか。

___

___

___

第12段落

12 Such steps should go hand in hand with measures to secure convenient daily transportation options for senior citizens who have to give up driving. These should include the distribution of discount coupons for buses and taxis, and the introduction of more low-cost public transport. Such measures will be strongly needed in rural depopulated areas where public transportation services such as buses are being cut back. Communities must strive to ensure that the transportation needs of local elderly residents who no longer drive can be met.

Words 下記の語彙について、その意味を調べましょう。

	語彙	品詞	意味
1	convenient	形容詞	
2	daily	形容詞	
3	option	名詞	
4	distribution	名詞	
5	community	名詞	
6	ensure	動詞	

Phrases 下記のフレーズについて、その意味を調べましょう。

	フレーズ	意味
1	go hand in hand with ~	
2	give up *doing*	
3	discount coupons	
4	low-cost public transport	
5	be strongly needed	
6	in rural depopulated areas	
7	cut back	
8	strive to *do*	
9	no longer	
10	meet the needs of ~	

Comprehension 本文の内容に即して、下記の質問に日本語で答えましょう。

1. 本文では、運転をやめた高齢者のために、どのような対策が提案されていますか。

2. 上記のような対策が、特に地方で必要とされているのは、なぜですか。

Writing Exercises

Phrase Writing
本文に登場するフレーズを参考にしながら、下記のフレーズを英訳しましょう。

	日本語のフレーズ	英語のフレーズ
1	6％の減少	
2	約200人の運転手	
3	8年ごとに	
4	2011年の時点で	
5	無料チケットの配布	

Sentence Writing
本文に登場する英文を参考にしながら、下記の和文を英訳しましょう。

1. その結果、交通死亡事故の件数は急激に減少した。

2. 政府は、このような交通規則の導入についても再考すべきである。

Vocabulary Building
下記のフレーズについて、意味が一致するものを線で結びましょう。

1. a food chain　　　・　　・梅雨
2. the rainy season　・　　・研究論文
3. salt damage　　　・　　・ビニール袋
4. natural resources　・　　・食物連鎖
5. the human body　 ・　　・塩害
6. a power plant　　 ・　　・天然資源
7. a plastic bag　　　・　　・人体
8. a research paper　・　　・発電所

[MEMO]

Unit 7
Tighten Measures to Combat Illegal Fishing (1)

Reading Passage

1 Japan has belatedly ratified an international agreement aimed at eliminating illegal fishing, which is estimated to reach up to 26 million tons a year and is feared to threaten efforts toward sustainable fishing in the world's oceans. As a major consumer of fish and a key fisheries player, Japan needs to tighten its own domestic measures against illegal, unreported and unregulated (IUU) fishing.

2 The Agreement on Port State Measures to Prevent, Deter and Eliminate Illegal, Unreported and Unregulated Fishing, brokered by the United Nations Food and Agriculture Organization (FAO), entered into force in June 2016 with the participation of more than 40 countries and the European Union. Due to the delay in readying domestic measures, it took Japan another year to ratify and join the agreement, which restricts port access to fishing ships that do not comply with the rules, including proof that they have proper operating licenses and disclosure of the species and quantity of the fish caught. It is meant to crack down on IUU fishing, whose value is said to amount each year to $23.5 billion worldwide, or roughly ¥2.6 trillion — far larger than Japan's annual fisheries output of some ¥1.5 trillion. It is feared that the products of IUU fishing are consumed in Japan in large volumes.

3 While ratification of the accord puts Japan in step with other countries in the concerted international effort to combat IUU fishing, a recent string of revelations of illicit fishing by Japanese fishermen exposes the nation's weak regulations against such practices.

4 Based on an agreement adopted by the Western and Central Pacific Fisheries Commission in 2015, the Fisheries Agency has introduced regulations on the catch of the threatened Pacific bluefin tuna — limiting the annual catch of immature fish weighing less than 30 kg to within 4,007 tons and setting catch quotas in each areas and method of fishing. But the government said in April that Japan already exceeded the annual limit through June, breaking the international commitment only two years after the regulation was introduced. The excess catch will be deducted from the quota for next year.

【347 words—*The Japan Times* (JUN 8, 2017)】

[Notes] illegal, unreported and unregulated (IUU) fishing: 違法・無報告・無規制で行われる漁業
The Agreement on Port State Measures to Prevent, Deter and Eliminate Illegal, Unreported and Unregulated Fishing: 違法・無報告・無規制漁業（IUU）の防止、抑制、廃絶のための寄港国措置協定（PSMA協定）
the United Nations Food and Agriculture Organization (FAO): 国連食糧農業機関
the Western and Central Pacific Fisheries Commission: 中西部太平洋まぐろ類委員会

第 1 段落

① Japan has belatedly ratified an international agreement aimed at eliminating illegal fishing, which is estimated to reach up to 26 million tons a year and is feared to threaten efforts toward sustainable fishing in the world's oceans. As a major consumer of fish and a key fisheries player, Japan needs to tighten its own domestic measures against illegal, unreported and unregulated (IUU) fishing.

Words 下記の語彙について、その意味を調べましょう。

	語彙	品詞	意味
1	belatedly	副詞	
2	ratify	動詞	
3	eliminate	動詞	
4	threaten	動詞	
5	effort	名詞	
6	consumer	名詞	
7	fishery	名詞	
8	tighten	動詞	
9	domestic	形容詞	
10	measure	名詞	
11	unreported	形容詞	
12	unregulated	形容詞	

Phrases 下記のフレーズについて、その意味を調べましょう。

	フレーズ	意味
1	an international agreement	
2	be aimed at ~	
3	illegal fishing	
4	be estimated to *do*	
5	up to 26 million tons	
6	be feared to *do*	
7	sustainable fishing	

Comprehension 本文の内容に即して、下記の質問に日本語で答えましょう。

1. 日本が批准した国際協定は、何を目的としたものですか。

2. そのような協定が批准された背景として、日本の漁業には、どのような現状がありますか。

第2段落

[2] The Agreement on Port State Measures to Prevent, Deter and Eliminate Illegal, Unreported and Unregulated Fishing, brokered by the United Nations Food and Agriculture Organization (FAO), entered into force in June 2016 with the participation of more than 40 countries and the European Union. Due to the delay in readying domestic measures, it took Japan another year to ratify and join the agreement, which restricts port access to fishing ships that do not comply with the rules, including proof that they have proper operating licenses and disclosure of the species and quantity of the fish caught. It is meant to crack down on IUU fishing, whose value is said to amount each year to $23.5 billion worldwide, or roughly ¥2.6 trillion — far larger than Japan's annual fisheries output of some ¥1.5 trillion. It is feared that the products of IUU fishing are consumed in Japan in large volumes.

Words 下記の語彙について、その意味を調べましょう。

	語彙	品詞	意味
1	prevent	動詞	
2	deter	動詞	
3	broker	動詞	
4	agriculture	名詞	
5	organization	名詞	
6	participation	名詞	
7	ready	動詞	
8	restrict	動詞	
9	proof	名詞	
10	proper	形容詞	
11	disclosure	名詞	
12	species	名詞	
13	quantity	名詞	
14	value	名詞	
15	billion	名詞	

16	worldwide	副詞	
17	roughly	副詞	
18	trillion	名詞	
19	annual	形容詞	
20	output	名詞	
21	product	名詞	
22	consume	動詞	

Phrases 下記のフレーズについて、その意味を調べましょう。

	フレーズ	意味
1	the United Nations	
2	enter into force	
3	the European Union	
4	due to ~	
5	delay in *doing*	
6	fishing ships	
7	comply with ~	
8	operating licenses	
9	crack down on ~	
10	amount to $23.5 billion	
11	each year	
12	it is feared that ---	
13	in large volumes	

Comprehension 本文の内容に即して、下記の質問に日本語で答えましょう。

1. 「違法・無報告・無規制漁業の防止、抑制、廃絶のための寄港国措置協定」の批准に日本が遅れたのは、なぜですか。

2. この協定により、日本に寄港する漁船に、どのようなことが求められるようになりましたか。

第3段落

[3] While ratification of the accord puts Japan in step with other countries in the concerted international effort to combat IUU fishing, a recent string of revelations of illicit fishing by Japanese fishermen exposes the nation's weak regulations against such practices.

Words 下記の語彙について、その意味を調べましょう。

	語彙	品詞	意味
1	ratification	名詞	
2	accord	名詞	
3	concerted	形容詞	
4	combat	動詞	
5	revelation	名詞	
6	illicit	形容詞	
7	fisherman	名詞	
8	expose	動詞	
9	regulation	名詞	

Phrases 下記のフレーズについて、その意味を調べましょう。

	フレーズ	意味
1	in step with ~	
2	a concerted effort	
3	a string of ~	
4	illicit fishing	

Comprehension 本文の内容に即して、下記の質問に日本語で答えましょう。

1. 日本の違法漁業に関して、本文にはどのようなことが書かれていますか。

_____
_____
_____
_____

[4] Based on an agreement adopted by the Western and Central Pacific Fisheries Commission in 2015, the Fisheries Agency has introduced regulations on the catch of the threatened Pacific bluefin tuna — limiting the annual catch of immature fish weighing less than 30 kg to within 4,007 tons and setting catch quotas in each areas and method of fishing. But the government said in April that Japan already exceeded the annual limit through June, breaking the international commitment only two years after the regulation was introduced. The excess catch will be deducted from the quota for next year.

Words 下記の語彙について、その意味を調べましょう。

	語彙	品詞	意味
1	adopt	動詞	
2	Pacific	形容詞	
3	commission	名詞	
4	introduce	動詞	
5	threatened	形容詞	
6	immature	形容詞	
7	weigh	動詞	
8	method	名詞	
9	exceed	動詞	
10	commitment	名詞	
11	excess	形容詞	

Phrases 下記のフレーズについて、その意味を調べましょう。

	フレーズ	意味
1	based on ~	
2	the Fisheries Agency	
3	Pacific Bluefin tuna	
4	limit X to Y	
5	an annual catch of fish	
6	less than 30 kg	
7	catch quotas	
8	a method of fishing	
9	the annual limit	
10	be deducted from ~	

Comprehension 本文の内容に即して、下記の質問に日本語で答えましょう。

1. クロマグロの捕獲に関して、水産庁が2015年に導入した規制とは、どのようなものですか。

2. 日本政府が4月に発表したこととは、どのようなことですか。

[MEMO]

Writing Exercises

Phrase Writing
本文に登場するフレーズを参考にしながら、下記のフレーズを英訳しましょう。

	日本語のフレーズ	英語のフレーズ
1	持続可能な農業	
2	太平洋	
3	水の量	
4	絶滅危惧種	
5	農法	

Sentence Writing
本文に登場する英文を参考にしながら、下記の和文を英訳しましょう。

1. この法律は、アワビの密漁を規制することを目的としている。

2. これらの天然資源は、世界中で大量に消費されている。

Vocabulary Building
下記のフレーズについて、意味が一致するものを線で結びましょう。

1. an oil field　　　・　　・物理法則
2. instant noodles　・　　・成虫
3. natural gas　　　・　　・希少金属
4. rare metals　　　・　　・油田
5. low-fat milk　　 ・　　・即席麺
6. frozen foods　　 ・　　・天然ガス
7. a physical law　 ・　　・低脂肪乳
8. adult insects　　・　　・冷凍食品

Unit 8
Tighten Measures to Combat Illegal Fishing (2)

*R*eading Passage

[5] It was revealed that unlicensed fishermen from Nagasaki Prefecture were catching bluefin tuna last year, while fishermen from Mie Prefecture were operating in defiance of Fisheries Agency requests for voluntary restraint in fishing. A subsequent probe exposed that fishermen from 12 prefectures were either catching bluefin tuna without a license or failing to report their catch — with the total catch of such illicit fishing reaching 132 tons, although the exposed illicit operations are believed to represent only a tip of the iceberg.

[6] Stock of Pacific bluefin tuna, a popular ingredient for sushi and other Japanese dishes, in waters near Japan is said to have fallen to some 17,000 tons as of 2014, or roughly one-tenth of its peak. Japan has caught more bluefin in the Pacific this year than any other country. Its lax enforcement of the fishing regulation could trigger international criticism and cast doubt on its credibility in the fight against IUU fishing.

[7] Illicit fishing is not limited to bluefin tuna. Cases of poaching of glass eel, sea cucumber and abalone by Japanese fishermen exposed by authorities are also reportedly rising in numbers.

[8] Illicit fishing remains rampant in Japan, it has been pointed out, because in many instances fishing regulations and the reporting of catches rely on voluntary compliance by fishermen, who face only weak punishments such as fines even when they are found to have been poaching. Lax enforcement of fishing regulations by Japan, one of the world's top consumers of fish, risks the nation becoming subject to greater international pressure to enact tighter regulations for the sake of preserving fish stocks.

[9] IUU fishing poses multiple risks for Japan's fisheries market, ranging from poaching by domestic fishermen and the exporting of their illicit catch to the import of fish illegally caught overseas. Domestic measures against IUU fishing need to be tightened. In ratifying the FAO agreement against illicit fishing, the United States, for example, reportedly decided to introduce a system requiring traders to prove that certain fish they handle, such as tuna and abalone — considered high IUU-risk species due to strong demand — have been caught in legitimate ways. Unless Japan introduces more powerful steps to crack down on IUU fishing, it could face criticism that its weak measures are compromising international efforts to combat this scourge.

【379 words—*The Japan Times* (JUN 8, 2017)】

第 5 段落

[5] It was revealed that unlicensed fishermen from Nagasaki Prefecture were catching bluefin tuna last year, while fishermen from Mie Prefecture were operating in defiance of Fisheries Agency requests for voluntary restraint in fishing. A subsequent probe exposed that fishermen from 12 prefectures were either catching bluefin tuna without a license or failing to report their catch — with the total catch of such illicit fishing reaching 132 tons, although the exposed illicit operations are believed to represent only a tip of the iceberg.

Words 下記の語彙について、その意味を調べましょう。

	語彙	品詞	意味
1	reveal	動詞	
2	unlicensed	形容詞	
3	prefecture	名詞	
4	operate	動詞	
5	voluntary	形容詞	
6	restraint	名詞	
7	subsequent	形容詞	
8	probe	名詞	
9	represent	動詞	

Phrases 下記のフレーズについて、その意味を調べましょう。

	フレーズ	意味
1	in defiance of ~	
2	fail to *do*	
3	the total catch of ~	
4	illicit operations	
5	be believed to *do*	
6	only a tip of iceberg	

Comprehension 本文の内容に即して、下記の質問に日本語で答えましょう。

1. 長崎県の漁師が犯した違法漁業とは、どのようなものですか。

2. 三重県の漁師が犯した違法漁業とは、どのようなものですか。

第6段落

⑥ Stock of Pacific bluefin tuna, a popular ingredient for sushi and other Japanese dishes, in waters near Japan is said to have fallen to some 17,000 tons as of 2014, or roughly one-tenth of its peak. Japan has caught more bluefin in the Pacific this year than any other country. Its lax enforcement of the fishing regulation could trigger international criticism and cast doubt on its credibility in the fight against IUU fishing.

Words 下記の語彙について、その意味を調べましょう。

	語彙	品詞	意味
1	stock	名詞	
2	ingredient	名詞	
3	lax	形容詞	
4	enforcement	名詞	
5	trigger	動詞	
6	criticism	名詞	
7	credibility	名詞	

Phrases 下記のフレーズについて、その意味を調べましょう。

	フレーズ	意味
1	Japanese dishes	
2	in waters near Japan	
3	be said to *do*	
4	fall to ~	
5	as of 2014	
6	one-tenth of its peak	
7	cast doubt on ~	

Comprehension 本文の内容に即して、下記の質問に日本語で答えましょう。

1. 日本近海では、クロマグロの乱獲は、どの程度進んでいますか。

2. 違法漁業の取り締まりが十分ではないことで、日本にはどのような影響が出てくると、本文には書かれていますか。

第7段落

[7] Illicit fishing is not limited to bluefin tuna. Cases of poaching of glass eel, sea cucumber and abalone by Japanese fishermen exposed by authorities are also reportedly rising in numbers.

Words 下記の語彙について、その意味を調べましょう。

	語彙	品詞	意味
1	case	名詞	
2	poaching	名詞	
3	eel	名詞	
4	cucumber	名詞	
5	abalone	名詞	
6	authority	名詞	
7	reportedly	副詞	

Phrases 下記のフレーズについて、その意味を調べましょう。

	フレーズ	意味
1	be not limited to ~	
2	glass eel	

| 3 | sea cucumber | |
| 4 | rise in numbers | |

Comprehension 本文の内容に即して、下記の質問に日本語で答えましょう。

1. 日本では、クロマグロの他に、どのような海産物の密猟が報告されていますか。

___

___

___

___

第 8 段落

[8] Illicit fishing remains rampant in Japan, it has been pointed out, because in many instances fishing regulations and the reporting of catches rely on voluntary compliance by fishermen, who face only weak punishments such as fines even when they are found to have been poaching. Lax enforcement of fishing regulations by Japan, one of the world's top consumers of fish, risks the nation becoming subject to greater international pressure to enact tighter regulations for the sake of preserving fish stocks.

Words 下記の語彙について、その意味を調べましょう。

	語彙	品詞	意味
1	remain	動詞	
2	rampant	形容詞	
3	compliance	名詞	
4	face	動詞	
5	punishment	名詞	
6	fine	名詞	
7	poach	動詞	
8	consumer	名詞	
9	pressure	名詞	
10	enact	動詞	
11	tight	形容詞	
12	preserve	動詞	

Phrases 下記のフレーズについて、その意味を調べましょう。

	フレーズ	意味
1	point out ~	
2	in many instances	
3	rely on ~	
4	become subject to ~	
5	for the sake of ~	
6	fish stocks	

Comprehension 本文の内容に即して、下記の質問に日本語で答えましょう。

1. 違法漁業が依然として日本に蔓延しているのは、なぜですか。

第 9 段落

⑨ IUU fishing poses multiple risks for Japan's fisheries market, ranging from poaching by domestic fishermen and the exporting of their illicit catch to the import of fish illegally caught overseas. Domestic measures against IUU fishing need to be tightened. In ratifying the FAO agreement against illicit fishing, the United States, for example, reportedly decided to introduce a system requiring traders to prove that certain fish they handle, such as tuna and abalone — considered high IUU-risk species due to strong demand — have been caught in legitimate ways. Unless Japan introduces more powerful steps to crack down on IUU fishing, it could face criticism that its weak measures are compromising international efforts to combat this scourge.

Words 下記の語彙について、その意味を調べましょう。

	語彙	品詞	意味
1	pose	動詞	
2	multiple	形容詞	
3	export	動詞	
4	import	名詞	
5	illegally	副詞	

6	overseas	副詞	
7	trader	名詞	
8	prove	動詞	
9	handle	動詞	
10	demand	名詞	
11	legitimate	形容詞	
12	unless	接続詞	
13	compromise	動詞	
14	scourge	名詞	

Phrases 下記のフレーズについて、その意味を調べましょう。

	フレーズ	意味
1	Japan's fisheries market	
2	range from X to Y	
3	require X to *do*	
4	high IUU-risk species	
5	due to ~	
6	in legitimate ways	
7	face criticism	

Comprehension 本文の内容に即して、下記の質問に日本語で答えましょう。

1. アメリカは、違法漁業を取り締まるために、どのようなシステムを導入しましたか。

---

2. 日本が違法漁業撲滅への対策を強化しない場合には、どのような批判を受けることになると、本文には書かれていますか。

Writing Exercises

Phrase Writing 本文に登場するフレーズを参考にしながら、下記のフレーズを英訳しましょう。

	日本語のフレーズ	英語のフレーズ
1	無免許医	
2	それらの5分の3	
3	シカの密猟	
4	批判にさらされる	
5	米の輸入	

Sentence Writing 本文に登場する英文を参考にしながら、下記の和文を英訳しましょう。

1. 違法な狩猟は、日本に限ったことではない。

2. 日本がこの協定を批准しない限り、違法漁業は蔓延状態のままとなるであろう。

Vocabulary Building 下記のフレーズについて、意味が一致するものを線で結びましょう。

1. a botanical garden　・　・赤血球
2. tropical rain forests　・　・地球科学
3. carbon monoxide　・　・代替エネルギー
4. food culture　・　・植物園
5. alternative energy　・　・一酸化炭素
6. earth science　・　・コーヒー豆
7. red blood cells　・　・食文化
8. coffee beans　・　・熱帯雨林

Scientists and Dual-Use Technologies (1)

Reading Passage

[1] The Science Council of Japan has released an interim report about its panel's discussions on whether it should amend or abandon its vow that scientists in Japan will not take part in military-purpose research. The discussions were spurred by the spread of dual-use technologies that can be used for both military and civilian purposes, as well as the launch of a Defense Ministry program to provide research funds to institutions for the development of dual-use technologies. On the question of whether scientists should take part in research whose results may be used for military purposes, the report only says that each university should examine the purpose, method and application of the research from technical and ethical viewpoints. The council should not only maintain its long-standing vow but also seriously consider how to uphold the autonomy and transparency of scientific research, which could be thrown in doubt by taking part in defense-related research.

[2] The SCJ was established in 1949 for the purpose of having the fruits of scientific research reflected in the nation's administration, industries and people's lives. Despite its position as a special organization under the Cabinet Office, it carries out its mission independently. Its 210 members represent some 840,000 researchers in such fields as natural science, engineering, social science and the humanities.

[3] In 1950, it declared a "firm determination" that scientists in Japan will never engage in research projects designed to achieve military purposes, reflecting on Japanese scientists' past cooperation with the government's war efforts. In 1967, it renewed the resolve by issuing a new statement, following the revelation that the U.S. military had provided funds to the Physical Society of Japan to help it hold an international conference the previous year.

[4] But last April, Takashi Onishi, president of Toyohashi University of Technology and chairman of the council, stated the view that scientists can take part in the Defense Ministry's program if the research results are used "within the bounds of self-defense." The budget set aside for the Defense Ministry program has rapidly increased since its launch in fiscal 2015. The amount doubled from ¥300 million in 2015 to ¥600 million in 2016, and the fiscal 2017 budget now before the Diet features ¥11 billion in such funds. Last May, the SCJ established the 15-member panel to discuss the matter. It plans to issue a final report in April.

[5] The panel's interim report issued in late January takes a cautious position over scientists' participation in research in the domain of "military security." It expresses concern over possible government intervention in the direction and confidentiality

of such research. As for the Defense Ministry's program, the report says the degree of government intervention in the research, including checks on its progress, will be high given that the program has the clear goal of using the research results for the development of defense equipment. 【472 words—*The Japan Times* (FEB 9, 2017)】

[Notes] The Science Council of Japan: 日本学術会議　the Physical Society of Japan: 日本物理学会
Takashi Onishi: 大西隆氏　Toyohashi University of Technology: 豊橋技術科学大学

① The Science Council of Japan has released an interim report about its panel's discussions on whether it should amend or abandon its vow that scientists in Japan will not take part in military-purpose research. The discussions were spurred by the spread of dual-use technologies that can be used for both military and civilian purposes, as well as the launch of a Defense Ministry program to provide research funds to institutions for the development of dual-use technologies. On the question of whether scientists should take part in research whose results may be used for military purposes, the report only says that each university should examine the purpose, method and application of the research from technical and ethical viewpoints. The council should not only maintain its long-standing vow but also seriously consider how to uphold the autonomy and transparency of scientific research, which could be thrown in doubt by taking part in defense-related research.

Words 下記の語彙について、その意味を調べましょう。

	語彙	品詞	意味
1	panel	名詞	
2	amend	動詞	
3	abandon	動詞	
4	vow	名詞	
5	spur	動詞	
6	spread	名詞	
7	launch	名詞	
8	institution	名詞	
9	method	名詞	
10	application	名詞	
11	maintain	動詞	
12	long-standing	形容詞	
13	seriously	副詞	
14	uphold	動詞	
15	autonomy	名詞	
16	transparency	名詞	

Phrases 下記のフレーズについて、その意味を調べましょう。

	フレーズ	意味
1	an interim report	
2	take part in ~	
3	military-purpose research	
4	dual-use technologies	
5	for civilian purposes	
6	the Defense Ministry	
7	research funds	
8	for military purposes	
9	from technical viewpoints	
10	from ethical viewpoints	
11	scientific research	
12	in doubt	
13	defense-related research	

Comprehension 本文の内容に即して、下記の質問に日本語で答えましょう。

1. 日本学術会議の委員会で検討されている問題とは、どのような問題のことですか。

2. 日本学術会議の委員会が発表した中間報告書には、どのようなことが述べられていると、本文には書かれていますか。

第 2 段落

[2] The SCJ was established in 1949 for the purpose of having the fruits of scientific research reflected in the nation's administration, industries and people's lives. Despite its position as a special organization under the Cabinet Office, it carries out its mission independently. Its 210 members represent some 840,000 researchers in such fields as natural science, engineering, social science and the humanities.

Words 下記の語彙について、その意味を調べましょう。

	語彙	品詞	意味
1	establish	動詞	
2	fruit	名詞	
3	administration	名詞	
4	industry	名詞	
5	position	名詞	
6	mission	名詞	
7	represent	動詞	
8	field	名詞	
9	engineering	名詞	

Phrases 下記のフレーズについて、その意味を調べましょう。

	フレーズ	意味
1	a special organization	
2	the Cabinet Office	
3	some 840,000 researchers	
4	natural science	
5	social science	
6	the humanities	

Comprehension 本文の内容に即して、下記の質問に日本語で答えましょう。

1. 日本学術会議は、どのような目的をもって設立されたと、本文には書かれていますか。

2. 日本学術会議を構成する210名の会員は、どのような役割を果たしていると、本文には書かれていますか。

第3段落

[3] In 1950, it declared a "firm determination" that scientists in Japan will never engage in research projects designed to achieve military purposes, reflecting on Japanese scientists' past cooperation with the government's war efforts. In 1967, it renewed the resolve by issuing a new statement, following the revelation that the U.S. military had provided funds to the Physical Society of Japan to help it hold an international conference the previous year.

Words 下記の語彙について、その意味を調べましょう。

	語彙	品詞	意味
1	declare	動詞	
2	cooperation	名詞	
3	renew	動詞	
4	resolve	名詞	
5	issue	動詞	
6	statement	名詞	
7	revelation	名詞	

Phrases 下記のフレーズについて、その意味を調べましょう。

	フレーズ	意味
1	a firm determination	
2	engage in ~	
3	research projects	
4	be designed to *do*	
5	reflect on ~	
6	the U.S. military	
7	hold an international conference	
8	the previous year	

Comprehension 本文の内容に即して、下記の質問に日本語で答えましょう。

1. 日本学術会議が1950年に行った決意表明とは、どのような決意表明のことですか。

第 **4** 段落

④ But last April, Takashi Onishi, president of Toyohashi University of Technology and chairman of the council, stated the view that scientists can take part in the Defense Ministry's program if the research results are used "within the bounds of self-defense." The budget set aside for the Defense Ministry program has rapidly increased since its launch in fiscal 2015. The amount doubled from ¥300 million in 2015 to ¥600 million in 2016, and the fiscal 2017 budget now before the Diet features ¥11 billion in such funds. Last May, the SCJ established the 15-member panel to discuss the matter. It plans to issue a final report in April.

Words 下記の語彙について、その意味を調べましょう。

	語彙	品詞	意味
1	president	名詞	
2	chairman	名詞	
3	state	動詞	
4	self-defense	名詞	
5	budget	名詞	
6	rapidly	副詞	
7	amount	名詞	
8	double	動詞	
9	million	名詞	
10	feature	動詞	
11	billion	名詞	
12	matter	名詞	

Phrases 下記のフレーズについて、その意味を調べましょう。

	フレーズ	意味
1	the view that ---	
2	research results	
3	within the bounds of ~	
4	set aside for ~	
5	in fiscal 2015	
6	the Diet	
7	plan to *do*	
8	a final report	

Comprehension 本文の内容に即して、下記の質問に日本語で答えましょう。

1. 昨年の4月に大西隆氏が述べた見解とは、どのような見解のことですか。

2. 防衛省のプログラムのために措置された予算について、本文にはどのようなことが述べられていますか。

第 5 段落

⑤ The panel's interim report issued in late January takes a cautious position over scientists' participation in research in the domain of "military security." It expresses concern over possible government intervention in the direction and confidentiality of such research. As for the Defense Ministry's program, the report says the degree of government intervention in the research, including checks on its progress, will be high given that the program has the clear goal of using the research results for the development of defense equipment.

Words 下記の語彙について、その意味を調べましょう。

	語彙	品詞	意味
1	participation	名詞	
2	domain	名詞	
3	intervention	名詞	
4	direction	名詞	
5	confidentiality	名詞	
6	degree	名詞	
7	progress	名詞	

Phrases 下記のフレーズについて、その意味を調べましょう。

	フレーズ	意味
1	in late January	
2	take a cautious position	
3	military security	
4	express concern	
5	as for ~	
6	given that ---	
7	defense equipment	

Comprehension 本文の内容に即して、下記の質問に日本語で答えましょう。

1. 軍事セキュリティ分野の研究に科学者が参画することに関して、委員会の中間報告書が慎重な立場を取っているのは、なぜですか。

[MEMO]

Writing Exercises

Phrase Writing
本文に登場するフレーズを参考にしながら、下記のフレーズを英訳しましょう。

	日本語のフレーズ	英語のフレーズ
1	教育上の目的で	
2	歴史的観点から	
3	2007 会計年度に	
4	常識の範囲内で	
5	10月下旬に	

Sentence Writing
本文に登場する英文を参考にしながら、下記の和文を英訳しましょう。

1. その委員会は、8月中旬に中間報告書を公表することにしている。

2. 他の科学者は、軍事目的の研究に関してさらに慎重な立場を取っている。

Vocabulary Building
下記のフレーズについて、意味が一致するものを線で結びましょう。

1. a chain reaction　・　　・天敵
2. empty cans　・　　・豆電球
3. forest fires　・　　・連鎖反応
4. unsalted butter　・　　・骨密度
5. air bubbles　・　　・森林火災
6. a miniature bulb　・　　・無塩バター
7. a natural enemy　・　　・気泡
8. bone density　・　　・空き缶

[MEMO]

Scientists and Dual-Use Technologies (2)

Reading Passage

[6] The report raises an important point — that it is difficult for scientists to control how their research results will be used. It notes that since scientists cannot completely control the "exit" of their research, they must make careful judgment at the "entrance." The report's warning applies to every kind of research, including research ostensibly for nonmilitary purposes. Scientists should realize that if they take part in research projects funded by the Defense Ministry, it will be all the more difficult or almost impossible for them to control the eventual application of their research results.

[7] In that context, the report says that while defense-related joint research by a business and an academic institution carries the risk of reduced transparency, the transparency of a Defense Ministry-funded project will be even lower due to much greater constraints placed on scientists concerning both the research process and the use of its results.

[8] The views of the council's members on the issue are reportedly mixed. SCJ chief Onishi himself is facing criticism for his position that appears to contradict the cautious stance in the report. A researcher at his university applied for the Defense Ministry program in 2015 with a proposal for research on the development of a gas mask, which was accepted. Onishi says there is nothing wrong with the research because a gas mask is not an offensive weapon and can also be used to protect workers at chemical plants in case of accidents. Some may agree that participation in the Defense Ministry program is justifiable if the research results are used for development of self-defense equipment. But they should heed the words of caution in the report that defensive and offensive-purpose military technologies are often inseparable — and that results of scientific research can be diverted to military purposes — including offensive ones — irrespective of scientists' intentions.

[9] Among SCJ members, opinions calling for changing or dropping the vow against defense-related research are said to be strong among natural science and engineering scholars. Behind this are the cuts in government research subsidies for universities, resulting in a shortage of research funds for natural science and engineering departments. The government has meanwhile decided to set up a panel at the Cabinet Office to discuss ways to expand research on dual-use technologies involving the Defense Ministry and other government organizations, academia and private-sector research institutions.

[10] Such policies combined threaten to distort the direction of Japan's scientific research. To support the healthy growth of scientific research, the government should change its direction and take steps to boost funds for research to improve people's lives—as the report

calls for. As it points out, expanded government spending on defense-related research could place a financial strain on pure academic research and hamper basic research.

【454 words—*The Japan Times* (FEB 9, 2017)】

第 段落　　　　　　　　　　　　　　　　　　　　　　　　　

6 The report raises an important point — that it is difficult for scientists to control how their research results will be used. It notes that since scientists cannot completely control the "exit" of their research, they must make careful judgment at the "entrance." The report's warning applies to every kind of research, including research ostensibly for nonmilitary purposes. Scientists should realize that if they take part in research projects funded by the Defense Ministry, it will be all the more difficult or almost impossible for them to control the eventual application of their research results.

Words 下記の語彙について、その意味を調べましょう。

	語彙	品詞	意味
1	raise	動詞	
2	note	動詞	
3	completely	副詞	
4	exit	名詞	
5	entrance	名詞	
6	warning	名詞	
7	ostensibly	副詞	
8	fund	動詞	
9	eventual	形容詞	
10	application	名詞	

Phrases 下記のフレーズについて、その意味を調べましょう。

	フレーズ	意味
1	make careful judgment	
2	apply to ~	
3	every kind of research	
4	all the more	
5	be almost impossible	

Comprehension 本文の内容に即して、下記の質問に日本語で答えましょう。

1. 中間報告書が浮き彫りにした1つの重要な論点とは、どのような論点のことですか。
___
___
___

第 7 段落

7 In that context, the report says that while defense-related joint research by a business and an academic institution carries the risk of reduced transparency, the transparency of a Defense Ministry-funded project will be even lower due to much greater constraints placed on scientists concerning both the research process and the use of its results.

Words 下記の語彙について、その意味を調べましょう。

	語彙	品詞	意味
1	context	名詞	
2	constraint	名詞	
3	concerning	前置詞	

Phrases 下記のフレーズについて、その意味を調べましょう。

	フレーズ	意味
1	joint research	
2	a business institution	
3	an academic institution	
4	due to ~	
5	place a constraint on ~	

Comprehension 本文の内容に即して、下記の質問に日本語で答えましょう。

1. 第7段落で述べられていることとは、どのようなことですか。
___
___
___
___
___

第8段落

[8] The views of the council's members on the issue are reportedly mixed. SCJ chief Onishi himself is facing criticism for his position that appears to contradict the cautious stance in the report. A researcher at his university applied for the Defense Ministry program in 2015 with a proposal for research on the development of a gas mask, which was accepted. Onishi says there is nothing wrong with the research because a gas mask is not an offensive weapon and can also be used to protect workers at chemical plants in case of accidents. Some may agree that participation in the Defense Ministry program is justifiable if the research results are used for development of self-defense equipment. But they should heed the words of caution in the report that defensive and offensive-purpose military technologies are often inseparable — and that results of scientific research can be diverted to military purposes — including offensive ones — irrespective of scientists' intentions.

Words 下記の語彙について、その意味を調べましょう。

	語彙	品詞	意味
1	reportedly	副詞	
2	criticism	名詞	
3	contradict	動詞	
4	proposal	名詞	
5	accept	動詞	
6	protect	動詞	
7	agree	動詞	
8	justifiable	形容詞	
9	heed	動詞	
10	caution	名詞	
11	defensive	形容詞	
12	offensive	形容詞	
13	inseparable	形容詞	
14	divert	動詞	
15	intention	名詞	

Phrases 下記のフレーズについて、その意味を調べましょう。

	フレーズ	意味
1	apply for ~	
2	a gas mask	
3	there is nothing wrong with ~	

4	an offensive weapon	
5	chemical plants	
6	in case of accidents	
7	self-defense equipment	
8	military technologies	
9	irrespective of ~	

Comprehension 本文の内容に即して、下記の質問に日本語で答えましょう。

1. 日本学術会議会長の大西氏は、ガスマスクの開発研究について、どのような見解をもっていますか。

2. 研究成果が自衛設備の開発のために利用される場合には、防衛省のプログラムに参画することは正当化されうるという議論に対して、中間報告書はどのような警告を発していますか。

第 9 段落

⑨ Among SCJ members, opinions calling for changing or dropping the vow against defense-related research are said to be strong among natural science and engineering scholars. Behind this are the cuts in government research subsidies for universities, resulting in a shortage of research funds for natural science and engineering departments. The government has meanwhile decided to set up a panel at the Cabinet Office to discuss ways to expand research on dual-use technologies involving the Defense Ministry and other government organizations, academia and private-sector research institutions.

Words 下記の語彙について、その意味を調べましょう。

	語彙	品詞	意味
1	scholar	名詞	
2	department	名詞	
3	meanwhile	副詞	
4	expand	動詞	

5	academia	名詞	
6	private-sector	形容詞	

Phrases 下記のフレーズについて、その意味を調べましょう。

	フレーズ	意味
1	call for *doing*	
2	research subsidies	
3	result in ~	
4	a shortage of research funds	
5	set up	
6	government organizations	
7	research institutions	

Comprehension 本文の内容に即して、下記の質問に日本語で答えましょう。

1. 防衛関連の研究を行わないという誓約を改めたり、あるいは破棄したりすることを求める意見が、自然科学や工学を専門とする研究者の間で優勢となっているのは、なぜですか。

___

第10段落

10 Such policies combined threaten to distort the direction of Japan's scientific research. To support the healthy growth of scientific research, the government should change its direction and take steps to boost funds for research to improve people's lives — as the report calls for. As it points out, expanded government spending on defense-related research could place a financial strain on pure academic research and hamper basic research.

Words 下記の語彙について、その意味を調べましょう。

	語彙	品詞	意味
1	policy	名詞	
2	distort	動詞	
3	healthy	形容詞	
4	boost	動詞	
5	spending	名詞	

6	financial	形容詞	
7	pure	形容詞	
8	hamper	動詞	

Phrases 下記のフレーズについて、その意味を調べましょう。

	フレーズ	意味
1	threaten to *do*	
2	take steps to *do*	
3	as the report calls for	
4	point out	
5	place a strain on ~	
6	academic research	
7	basic research	

Comprehension 本文の内容に即して、下記の質問に日本語で答えましょう。

1. 科学研究の健全な発展を支援していくために、政府がすべきこととして、中間報告書はどのようなことを求めていますか。

2. 政府が防衛関連の研究に多くの予算を割くことで、どのようなことが起こってくると、本文には書かれていますか。

Writing Exercises

Phrase Writing
本文に登場するフレーズを参考にしながら、下記のフレーズを英訳しましょう。

	日本語のフレーズ	英語のフレーズ
1	あらゆる種類の物質	
2	大雨のために	
3	核兵器	
4	水不足	
5	応用研究	

Sentence Writing
本文に登場する英文を参考にしながら、下記の和文を英訳しましょう。

1. 日本政府は、科学研究の健全な発展を支援していくべきである。

2. 報告書が指摘するように、研究費不足は最も切実な問題の1つである。

Vocabulary Building
下記のフレーズについて、意味が一致するものを線で結びましょう。

1. desertification　　・　　・虫刺され
2. an oxygen atom　　・　　・火山灰
3. a blood test　　・　　・動物心理学
4. insect bites　　・　　・砂漠化
5. draft beer　　・　　・血液検査
6. volcanic ash　　・　　・酸素原子
7. animal psychology　　・　　・大気汚染
8. air pollution　　・　　・生ビール

Human Genome Editing (1)

Reading Passage

1. A type of genetic engineering called genome editing is receiving worldwide attention as a technique that can produce amazing progress in medicine and improvement of agricultural products. But the technique, which precisely alters genetic sequences, has raised ethical and social questions. Given the move to strongly push research on genome editing in Japan, including human genome editing, it is imperative that the government and academic societies concerned work out strict rules because the technique at this stage is not fully reliable and its ethical, legal and social ramifications are not completely known.

2. In genome editing, targeted DNA in a cell is cut away at a specific location to inactivate a problematic gene or to insert a replacement DNA sequence for replacement or repairs in order to produce a desired result. While DNA is a substance that contains genes, a genome refers to the entirety of hereditary information contained in genes and chromosomes in cells. In humans, a copy of the entire genome — more than 3 billion DNA base pairs — is contained in all cells that have a nucleus. Since the accuracy of genome editing at present is not high enough and inaccurate editing can happen, there is a view that genome editing is not an established technique. The current mainstream method in genome editing is programming a complex made up of a guide RNA and a certain type of protein to target a problematic gene in DNA.

3. In April last year, news that Chinese scientists edited the DNA of human embryos — the first time this has been done — shocked the world and touched off a debate because of the ethical implication of such endeavors. A team of researchers at Sun Yat-sen University in Guangzhou injected 86 nonviable embryos with a complex called CRISPR/Cas 9 to modify the gene responsible for beta thalassemia, a fatal blood disorder. Of the embryos, 71 survived and 54 of them were genetically tested. It was found that just 28 were successfully spliced, but that only a fraction of them contained the replacement genetic material. The researchers also detected a number of "off-target" mutations apparently caused by the injection of the CRISPR/Cas 9 complex.

4. Apparently prompted by what the Chinese team did, the Cabinet Office's life ethics study group of experts in April issued an interim report that condoned basic genome editing research on manipulating genes in fertilized human embryos but said returning an embryo whose problematic gene has been modified through genome editing to a womb is not acceptable. The Science Council of Japan in July started discussions by a committee of specialists on issues related to medical research and treatment that applies genome editing to fertilized human embryos and reproductive cells, and plans to issue a report

or proposal by fall 2017. Early this month, the Japanese Society for Genome Editing issued a statement that basically agreed with the government study group's position.

【479 words—*The Japan Times* (SEP 26, 2016)】

[Notes] a guide RNA: ガイド RNA
Sun Yat-sen University: 中山（ちゅうざん）大学または孫逸仙（そんいっせん）大学
Guangzhou: 広州　CRISPR/Cas 9: 遺伝子改変技術の名称　a study group of experts: 専門調査会
The Science Council of Japan: 日本学術会議
the Japanese Society for Genome Editing: 日本ゲノム編集学会

第 1 段落

[1] A type of genetic engineering called genome editing is receiving worldwide attention as a technique that can produce amazing progress in medicine and improvement of agricultural products. But the technique, which precisely alters genetic sequences, has raised ethical and social questions. Given the move to strongly push research on genome editing in Japan, including human genome editing, it is imperative that the government and academic societies concerned work out strict rules because the technique at this stage is not fully reliable and its ethical, legal and social ramifications are not completely known.

Words 下記の語彙について、その意味を調べましょう。

	語彙	品詞	意味
1	worldwide	形容詞	
2	amazing	形容詞	
3	progress	名詞	
4	medicine	名詞	
5	improvement	名詞	
6	precisely	副詞	
7	alter	動詞	
8	ethical	形容詞	
9	legal	形容詞	
10	ramification	名詞	

Phrases 下記のフレーズについて、その意味を調べましょう。

	フレーズ	意味
1	genetic engineering	
2	genome editing	
3	agricultural products	
4	genetic sequences	

5	raise questions	
6	given ~	
7	human genome editing	
8	it is imperative that ---	
9	the academic societies concerned	
10	work out	
11	strict rules	
12	at this stage	
13	be fully reliable	
14	be not completely known	

Comprehension 本文の内容に即して、下記の質問に日本語で答えましょう。

1. ゲノム編集と呼ばれる技術が抱える問題点として、本文ではどのようなことが指摘されていますか。

第 2 段落

2 In genome editing, targeted DNA in a cell is cut away at a specific location to inactivate a problematic gene or to insert a replacement DNA sequence for replacement or repairs in order to produce a desired result. While DNA is a substance that contains genes, a genome refers to the entirety of hereditary information contained in genes and chromosomes in cells. In humans, a copy of the entire genome — more than 3 billion DNA base pairs — is contained in all cells that have a nucleus. Since the accuracy of genome editing at present is not high enough and inaccurate editing can happen, there is a view that genome editing is not an established technique. The current mainstream method in genome editing is programming a complex made up of a guide RNA and a certain type of protein to target a problematic gene in DNA.

Words 下記の語彙について、その意味を調べましょう。

	語彙	品詞	意味
1	cell	名詞	
2	inactivate	動詞	

3	problematic	形容詞	
4	gene	名詞	
5	insert	動詞	
6	sequence	名詞	
7	replacement	名詞	
8	repair	名詞	
9	substance	名詞	
10	genome	名詞	
11	entirety	名詞	
12	chromosome	名詞	
13	billion	名詞	
14	nucleus	名詞	
15	accuracy	名詞	
16	inaccurate	形容詞	
17	established	形容詞	
18	current	形容詞	
19	mainstream	形容詞	
20	method	名詞	
21	program	動詞	
22	complex	名詞	
23	target	動詞	

Phrases 下記のフレーズについて、その意味を調べましょう。

	フレーズ	意味
1	targeted DNA	
2	cut away	
3	at a specific location	
4	refer to ~	
5	hereditary information	
6	the entire genome	
7	base pairs	
8	at present	
9	there is a view that ---	
10	be made up of ~	
11	a certain type of protein	

Comprehension 本文の内容に即して、下記の質問に日本語で答えましょう。

1. ゲノム編集と呼ばれる技術では、具体的にはどのようなことが可能になると、本文には書かれていますか。

2. 本文では、「ゲノム」という概念をどのように定義していますか。

3. 現在主流となっているゲノム編集の方法とは、どのようなものですか。

第 3 段落

[3] In April last year, news that Chinese scientists edited the DNA of human embryos — the first time this has been done — shocked the world and touched off a debate because of the ethical implication of such endeavors. A team of researchers at Sun Yat-sen University in Guangzhou injected 86 nonviable embryos with a complex called CRISPR/Cas 9 to modify the gene responsible for beta thalassemia, a fatal blood disorder. Of the embryos, 71 survived and 54 of them were genetically tested. It was found that just 28 were successfully spliced, but that only a fraction of them contained the replacement genetic material. The researchers also detected a number of "off-target" mutations apparently caused by the injection of the CRISPR/Cas 9 complex.

Words 下記の語彙について、その意味を調べましょう。

	語彙	品詞	意味
1	edit	動詞	
2	embryo	名詞	
3	implication	名詞	
4	endeavor	名詞	

5	nonviable	形容詞	
6	modify	動詞	
7	fatal	形容詞	
8	splice	動詞	
9	detect	動詞	
10	apparently	副詞	
11	injection	名詞	

Phrases 下記のフレーズについて、その意味を調べましょう。

	フレーズ	意味
1	touch off a debate	
2	inject X with Y	
3	be responsible for ~	
4	beta thalassemia	
5	a blood disorder	
6	be genetically tested	
7	it was found that ---	
8	only a fraction of them	
9	genetic material	
10	a number of ~	
11	off-target mutations	
12	be caused by ~	

Comprehension 本文の内容に即して、下記の質問に日本語で答えましょう。

1. ヒト胚の DNA を用いて、中国の研究者チームが行ったこととは、どのようなことですか。

_____
_____
_____
_____
_____
_____

第 4 段落

4 Apparently prompted by what the Chinese team did, the Cabinet Office's life ethics study group of experts in April issued an interim report that condoned basic genome editing research on manipulating genes in fertilized human embryos but said returning an embryo whose problematic gene has been modified through genome editing to a womb is not acceptable. The Science Council of Japan in July started discussions by a committee of specialists on issues related to medical research and treatment that applies genome editing to fertilized human embryos and reproductive cells, and plans to issue a report or proposal by fall 2017. Early this month, the Japanese Society for Genome Editing issued a statement that basically agreed with the government study group's position.

Words 下記の語彙について、その意味を調べましょう。

	語彙	品詞	意味
1	apparently	副詞	
2	prompt	動詞	
3	issue	動詞	
4	condone	動詞	
5	manipulate	動詞	
6	womb	名詞	
7	acceptable	形容詞	
8	statement	名詞	
9	basically	副詞	
10	position	名詞	

Phrases 下記のフレーズについて、その意味を調べましょう。

	フレーズ	意味
1	the Cabinet Office	
2	life ethics	
3	an interim report	
4	fertilized human embryos	
5	a committee of specialists	
6	be related to ~	
7	medical research	
8	medical treatment	
9	apply X to Y	
10	reproductive cells	
11	early this month	
12	agree with ~	

Comprehension 本文の内容に即して、下記の質問に日本語で答えましょう。

1. 内閣府の生命倫理専門調査会によって発行された中間報告書には、ゲノム編集に関して、どのような見解が述べられてあると、本文には書かれていますか。

2. 日本学術会議の専門家委員会が7月に開始したこととは、どのようなことですか。

[MEMO]

Writing Exercises

Phrase Writing
本文に登場するフレーズを参考にしながら、下記のフレーズを英訳しましょう。

	日本語のフレーズ	英語のフレーズ
1	土木工学	
2	関連情報	
3	多数の研究者	
4	精神疾患	
5	がん細胞	

Sentence Writing
本文に登場する英文を参考にしながら、下記の和文を英訳しましょう。

1. DNA は、遺伝子を含む物質として、一般に定義することができる。

2. ゲノム編集として知られる技術は、様々な倫理上の問題を提起してきた。

Vocabulary Building
下記のフレーズについて、意味が一致するものを線で結びましょう。

1. carbon dioxide ・　　　　・ 化石燃料
2. acid rain ・　　　　・ 生物濃縮
3. climate change ・　　　　・ 食物アレルギー
4. a food allergy ・　　　　・ 完全燃焼
5. complete combustion ・　　　　・ 気候変動
6. fossil fuels ・　　　　・ 二酸化炭素
7. bioaccumulation ・　　　　・ 塩の結晶
8. salt crystals ・　　　　・ 酸性雨

[MEMO]

Human Genome Editing (2)

Reading Passage

⑤ The government study group, composed of 15 experts on life sciences, law and ethics, specifically said that basic research is acceptable for such purposes as finding out the roles played by genes at an early stage of embryonic development with the help of genome editing, developing methods to treat congenital hard-to-cure diseases and improving assisted reproductive technologies. But it called on researchers to limit their research to the first two weeks of a human embryo's development and to dispose of such embryos after their research is over. It also said that researchers should consider whether it is possible to use animal embryos instead of human embryos.

⑥ The group flatly turned down clinical use of human genome editing at this stage, citing the risks of inaccurate or incomplete editing such as off-target mutations and mosaicism or interminglement of modified and unmodified genes, as well as the difficulty to predict what effects gene alteration will have on other genes and to examine risks that future generations may face as a result of genetic alterations in embryos that will be passed from generation to generation.

⑦ Because the group's report has no binding power, the possibility cannot be ruled out that ethics committees of research institutes could permit human genome editing research beyond the scope mentioned by the report. The government and academic societies need to start working to develop binding guidelines or legal regulations that control human genome editing research by fully taking into consideration not only the ethical but also the social problems the technique can cause.

⑧ An international summit on human gene editing held in December in Washington, hosted by the U.S. National Academy of Sciences, the U.S. National Academy of Medicine, the Chinese Academy of Sciences and Britain's Royal Society, issued an statement which pointed out that "permanent genetic 'enhancements' to subsets of the population could exacerbate social inequalities or be used coercively." The statement stressed that "it would be irresponsible to proceed with any clinical use of germ-line editing" unless the relevant safety and efficacy issues are solved by fully weighing risks, potential benefits and alternatives, and unless there is broad societal consensus about the appropriateness of the proposed application. It also called for putting all clinical use of human genome editing "under appropriate regulatory oversight."

⑨ Human genome editing could have serious consequences depending on the level of its reliability and the way it is used. Theoretically it is even possible to use the technique to produce "designer babies."

10 The government study group's decision to make a manual to oversee the clinical use of human genome editing is meaningful. But given the technique's potential benefits and risks, which are both of great consequence, there is a strong need for a wide range of the public, including ordinary citizens, lawmakers, bureaucrats, scientists, and legal and ethics experts, to carry out informed and detailed discussions so that human genome editing can truly contribute to enhancing the well-being of all people.

【489 words—*The Japan Times* (SEP 26, 2016)】

[Notes] the U.S. National Academy of Sciences: 米国科学アカデミー
the U.S. National Academy of Medicine: 米国医学アカデミー
the Chinese Academy of Sciences: 中国科学院　　Britain's Royal Society: 英国王立協会

第 5 段落

5 The government study group, composed of 15 experts on life sciences, law and ethics, specifically said that basic research is acceptable for such purposes as finding out the roles played by genes at an early stage of embryonic development with the help of genome editing, developing methods to treat congenital hard-to-cure diseases and improving assisted reproductive technologies. But it called on researchers to limit their research to the first two weeks of a human embryo's development and to dispose of such embryos after their research is over. It also said that researchers should consider whether it is possible to use animal embryos instead of human embryos.

Words 下記の語彙について、その意味を調べましょう。

	語彙	品詞	意味
1	expert	名詞	
2	ethics	名詞	
3	specifically	副詞	
4	purpose	名詞	
5	congenital	形容詞	

Phrases 下記のフレーズについて、その意味を調べましょう。

	フレーズ	意味
1	be composed of ~	
2	life sciences	
3	basic research	
4	at an early stage of ~	
5	embryonic development	
6	with the help of ~	

7	hard-to-cure diseases	
8	assisted reproductive technologies	
9	call on X to *do*	
10	limit X to Y	
11	the first two weeks	
12	a human embryo	
13	dispose of ~	
14	animal embryos	
15	instead of ~	

Comprehension 本文の内容に即して、下記の質問に日本語で答えましょう。

1. ヒトゲノム編集に関して、政府の専門調査会が容認可能としたこととは、どのようなことですか。

2. ヒトゲノム編集の基礎研究を行う上で、政府の専門調査会が研究者に求めたこととして、本文には3つのことが述べられていますが、その3つのこととは、どのようなことですか。

第 6 段落

⑥ The group flatly turned down clinical use of human genome editing at this stage, citing the risks of inaccurate or incomplete editing such as off-target mutations and mosaicism or interminglement of modified and unmodified genes, as well as the difficulty to predict what effects gene alteration will have on other genes and to examine risks that future generations may face as a result of genetic alterations in embryos that will be passed from generation to generation.

Words 下記の語彙について、その意味を調べましょう。

	語彙	品詞	意味
1	flatly	副詞	
2	clinical	形容詞	
3	cite	動詞	

4	incomplete	形容詞	
5	mosaicism	名詞	
6	predict	動詞	
7	face	動詞	
8	pass	動詞	

Phrases 下記のフレーズについて、その意味を調べましょう。

	フレーズ	意味
1	turn down	
2	clinical use	
3	at this stage	
4	modified genes	
5	unmodified genes	
6	gene alteration	
7	have an effect on ~	
8	future generations	
9	as a result of ~	
10	from generation to generation	

Comprehension 本文の内容に即して、下記の質問に日本語で答えましょう。

1. 政府の専門調査会がヒトゲノム編集の臨床使用について一切承認しなかった理由として、本文では3つのことが述べられていますが、その3つのこととは、どのようなことですか。

第 ⑦ 段落

⑦ Because the group's report has no binding power, the possibility cannot be ruled out that ethics committees of research institutes could permit human genome editing research beyond the scope mentioned by the report. The government and academic societies need to start working to develop binding guidelines or legal regulations that control human genome editing research by fully taking into consideration not only the ethical but also the social problems the technique can cause.

Words 下記の語彙について、その意味を調べましょう。

	語彙	品詞	意味
1	possibility	名詞	
2	permit	動詞	
3	scope	名詞	
4	mention	動詞	
5	binding	形容詞	
6	guideline	名詞	
7	fully	副詞	

Phrases 下記のフレーズについて、その意味を調べましょう。

	フレーズ	意味
1	have no binding power	
2	rule out	
3	an ethics committee	
4	a research institute	
5	academic societies	
6	legal regulations	
7	take ~ into consideration	

Comprehension 本文の内容に即して、下記の質問に日本語で答えましょう。

1. 政府の専門調査会による報告書を踏まえて、今後必要となってくることとは、どのようなことですか。

___

___

___

___

第8段落

[8] An international summit on human gene editing held in December in Washington, hosted by the U.S. National Academy of Sciences, the U.S. National Academy of Medicine, the Chinese Academy of Sciences and Britain's Royal Society, issued an statement which pointed out that "permanent genetic 'enhancements' to subsets of the population could exacerbate social inequalities or be used coercively." The statement stressed that "it would be irresponsible to proceed with any clinical use of germ-line

editing" unless the relevant safety and efficacy issues are solved by fully weighing risks, potential benefits and alternatives, and unless there is broad societal consensus about the appropriateness of the proposed application. It also called for putting all clinical use of human genome editing "under appropriate regulatory oversight."

Words 下記の語彙について、その意味を調べましょう。

	語彙	品詞	意味
1	host	動詞	
2	permanent	形容詞	
3	enhancement	名詞	
4	subset	名詞	
5	exacerbate	動詞	
6	coercively	副詞	
7	stress	動詞	
8	irresponsible	形容詞	
9	germ-line	名詞	
10	relevant	形容詞	
11	efficacy	名詞	
12	weigh	動詞	
13	alternative	名詞	
14	societal	形容詞	
15	consensus	名詞	
16	appropriateness	名詞	
17	application	名詞	
18	appropriate	形容詞	
19	regulatory	形容詞	
20	oversight	名詞	

Phrases 下記のフレーズについて、その意味を調べましょう。

	フレーズ	意味
1	an international summit	
2	be held	
3	point out	
4	social inequalities	
5	proceed with ~	
6	potential benefits	
7	call for *doing*	

Comprehension 本文の内容に即して、下記の質問に日本語で答えましょう。

1. ワシントンで12月に開催された国際サミットでは、ヒトの遺伝子編集技術に関して、3つのことが指摘されたと本文には書かれていますが、その3つのこととは、どのようなことですか。

___
___
___
___
___
___

第9段落

⑨ Human genome editing could have serious consequences depending on the level of its reliability and the way it is used. Theoretically it is even possible to use the technique to produce "designer babies."

第10段落

⑩ The government study group's decision to make a manual to oversee the clinical use of human genome editing is meaningful. But given the technique's potential benefits and risks, which are both of great consequence, there is a strong need for a wide range of the public, including ordinary citizens, lawmakers, bureaucrats, scientists, and legal and ethics experts, to carry out informed and detailed discussions so that human genome editing can truly contribute to enhancing the well-being of all people.

Words 下記の語彙について、その意味を調べましょう。

	語彙	品詞	意味
1	serious	形容詞	
2	consequence	名詞	
3	reliability	名詞	
4	theoretically	副詞	
5	manual	名詞	
6	oversee	動詞	
7	meaningful	形容詞	
8	lawmaker	名詞	
9	bureaucrat	名詞	
10	informed	形容詞	

11	detailed	形容詞	
12	truly	副詞	
13	enhance	動詞	
14	well-being	名詞	

Phrases 下記のフレーズについて、その意味を調べましょう。

	フレーズ	意味
1	depending on ~	
2	designer babies	
3	given ~	
4	be of great consequence	
5	a wide range of ~	
6	the public	
7	ordinary citizens	
8	legal experts	
9	carry out discussions	
10	contribute to *doing*	

Comprehension 本文の内容に即して、下記の質問に日本語で答えましょう。

1. 第9段落で述べられていることとは、どのようなことですか。

2. ヒトゲノム編集の臨床使用について考えていく際に、強く望まれていることとは、どのようなことですか。

Writing Exercises

Phrase Writing
本文に登場するフレーズを参考にしながら、下記のフレーズを英訳しましょう。

	日本語のフレーズ	英語のフレーズ
1	最後の3か月	
2	次世代技術	
3	説明力がない	
4	国際会議	
5	多種多様な野菜	

Sentence Writing
本文に登場する英文を参考にしながら、下記の和文を英訳しましょう。

1. 実際には、上述の指針を無視することさえ可能である。

2. このような場合には、以下の可能性を除外することができない。

Vocabulary Building
下記のフレーズについて、意味が一致するものを線で結びましょう。

1. deforestation　　　　　　　・　　・絶滅危惧種
2. cell division　　　　　　　・　　・発酵食品
3. static electricity　　　　　・　　・森林破壊
4. an endangered species　・　　・細胞分裂
5. soil erosion　　　　　　　　・　　・絶滅動物
6. an evolutionary tree　　　・　　・静電気
7. an extinct animal　　　　　・　　・土壌浸食
8. fermented foods　　　　　　・　　・系統樹

音声ファイルのダウンロード方法

英宝社ホームページ (http://www.eihosha.co.jp/) の
「テキスト音声ダウンロード」バナーをクリックすると、
音声ファイルダウンロードページにアクセスすることができます。

Reading Contemporary Society through Editorials
英語社説で読み解く現代社会

2019年1月15日　初　版
2023年3月31日　2　刷

編著者ⓒ　安　原　和　也
　　　　　鬼　頭　　　修

発行者　　佐　々　木　　元

発行所　株式会社　英　宝　社
〒 101-0032 東京都千代田区岩本町2-7-7
Tel [03] (5833) 5870　Fax [03] (5833) 5872

ISBN 978-4-269-18051-2 C1082
［製版：㈱マナ・コムレード／表紙デザイン：伊谷企画／印刷製本：日本ハイコム㈱］

本書の一部または全部を、コピー、スキャン、デジタル化等での無断複写・複製は、著作権法上での例外を除き禁じられています。本書を代行業者等の第三者に依頼してのスキャンやデジタル化は、たとえ個人や家庭内での利用であっても著作権侵害となり、著作権法上一切認められておりません。